FIND YOUR PEOPLE

**Building Deep Community
in a Lonely World**

A STUDY IN 7 SESSIONS

Jennie Allen

H Harper*Christian*
Resources

CONTENTS

WHAT DO YOU HOPE TO GET OUT OF THIS STUDY?

_____

_____

_____

_____

GET HONEST

This is going to get messy, but it will be worth it. We will be dealing with the things that make us most vulnerable to other people, and the things that make us lonely. God wants to do something with that. But until we recognize that we are in need of Him, and in need of others, we will miss what He has for us. If you are craving the idea of finding your people, perhaps you would be willing to consider a way to deeper relationships, even if it is costly. Be honest with yourself and honest with God. He knows all of it already anyway.

ENGAGE WITH YOUR SMALL GROUP

In a study all about God's plan for community, your community is going to be essential. You have kindred warriors at your side, fighting with you and for you. Pray, speak truth in love, and encourage each other to open up and be real. Be vulnerable and do not abandon those who are vulnerable with you. Prepare to go to war alongside these women. Keep your group a safe place to wrestle and discover and also a place filled with truth. John describes Christ as being "full of grace and truth" (John 1:14). I pray that this is how your small group will be described.

"And you shall know the truth, and the truth shall make you free". (John 8:32 NKJV)

COMMIT TO BEING CONSISTENT AND PRESENT

Commit to being present at your group meetings, barring an emergency, and arrange your schedule so you do not miss any part in this journey. Have your lesson and projects finished when you come to the group meeting (except for this one, of course).

GROUND RULES FOR GROUP DISCUSSION

BE CONCISE.

Share your answers to the questions while protecting others' time for sharing. Be thoughtful. Don't be afraid to share with the group; but try not to dominate the conversation.

"Everyone should be quick to listen, slow to speak". (James 1:19)

KEEP GROUP MEMBERS' STORIES CONFIDENTIAL.

Many things your group members share are things they are choosing to share with *you*, not with your husband or other friends. Protect each other by not allowing anything shared in the group to leave the group.

RELY ON SCRIPTURE FOR TRUTH.

We are prone to use conventional, worldly wisdom as truth. While there is value in that, this is not the place. If you feel led to respond, please only respond with God's truth and Word, not "advice."

NO COUNSELING.

Protect the group by not directing all attention on solving one person's problem. This is the place for confessing and discovery and applying truth together as a group. Your group leader will be able to direct you to more help outside the group time if you need it. Don't be afraid to ask for help.

STUDY DESIGN

For Group Study: In the first meeting, your group's study guides will be passed out and you will work through the Introduction lesson together. You will watch the video teaching as a group and have discussion based on the Conversation Cards as well.

For Independent Study: Each video teaching is included with your study guide. Simply follow the instructions on the inside cover for access to all the video sessions.

After the first week, each session in the study guide is meant to be completed on your own during the week before coming to the group meeting. These lessons may feel different from studies you have done in the past. They are very interactive. The beginning of each session will involve you, your Bible, and a pen, working through Scripture and listening to God's voice. Each session includes four projects you can do to further process how to live God's Word.

Don't feel as if each study has to be finished in one sitting; take a few blocks of time throughout the week if you need to. The goal of this study is to dig deeply into Scripture and uncover how it applies to your life, *to deeply engage the mind and the heart*. Projects, stories, and Bible study all play a role in it. You may be drawing or journaling or interacting with others in your community. At each group meeting you will discuss your experience in working through that week's material.

WHAT THIS STUDY IS NOT

We all are products of messed-up environments. Even with the best parents, spouses, and friends, we still have wounds from relationships. The hurt from these relationships takes work to process, and there are many great resources your group leader can suggest that take you deeper into the wounds from your past. I believe in the wisdom of Christian counseling, and there is a time and place for it. Christian counseling is a process I went through earlier in my life, and it truly brought so much freedom.

However, in this study the focus is intended to remain on God and His plan for us as a thriving community. I believe growing in our perspective of who He is and what He has for us changes the way we view our past hurts and current struggles.

"He heals the brokenhearted and binds up their wounds". (Psalm 147:3 NKJV)

Nothing is more powerful than God getting bigger in our lives. He has the power to heal with a word. My goal as you walk through *Find Your People* is that God would get bigger for you and as He does, you would see a new way to do life, with others, and never alone.

SESSION 1

INTRODUCTION

Before this study was a study, it was a question. In fact, it was the number-one question I've gotten from you all throughout the years. And it's a big one: *How do I make friends as an adult?*

Of all the struggles we go through, this is the one that comes back over and over again because, let's face it: we've all felt that loneliness. Especially living in our spread-out world, which seems tailor-made for isolation and individualism. We're wondering: *How do I get deep with someone? How do I build trust with someone? Why is finding and keeping my people so difficult?*

And the kicker:

Why do I live lonely?

It's a question that hurts to ask, because so many of us would answer that question with, *There's something wrong with me. I must be defective.* Or, *Because it's the only safe way.*

But listen. It's not just you. This secret hurt and frustration is not so secret anymore. In this study, we're going to shine God's light on this place where we might otherwise remain in the dark—sad and isolated and missing out. We'll seek out His plan for thriving instead of settling for surface and shallow. But first I want you to know:

You're not alone in feeling alone.

When I first started doing my podcast way back in 2016, the whole first season was about loneliness. I wanted to hit this topic out of the gate because it was clear it was at the front of so many minds, and there had to be something we could do about this together.

So I asked people to email me, and answer, straight up:

Why is finding and keeping your people so hard? Why do we live lonely?

And these were some of the answers:

"I reach out, but people can't come over. They are too busy. I finally stopped asking." **–Amanda**

"After being burnt, backstabbed, lied to, and betrayed, I have a hard time letting people inside my walls." **–Patti**

"I don't know how to get past the 'getting to know you' small talk." **–Emily**

"I feel like a burden so I just don't go deep." **–Molly**

"I feel like I have to pretend that I am okay or be judged." **–Stefanie**

"I have expectations of what I think 'my people' should be and they don't measure up." **–Sandra**

"I'm afraid I might need more than I can give." **–Kim**

"I'm too exhausted from being a mom, wife, employee to be a good friend." **–Kennedy**

"Staying friends after an argument is just too awkward. I don't know how to move past it." **–Ella**

"To be honest, it's easier to do it by myself." **–Ashley**

Does any of this sound familiar to you?

I know it does to me.

And for a staggering number of people.

In 2020, the pandemic opened a lot of our eyes to what we were lacking and missing in our relationships. But even before 2020, when people were sharing their stories with me, the pandemic of loneliness was in full swing. Taking us out. Killing our joy. Killing us physically and mentally. For so many of us, that ache has been there so long that you wonder if it is just the human condition and has no chance of going away.

But I don't think this is the case. I think, in this moment, something is being revealed to us: when it comes to community there is something fundamentally wrong with how we have built our lives.

We tuck into our little residences with our little family or our roommates or alone, staring at our little screens. We never want to trouble our neighbors for anything, so we build a small little crevice in the world with everything we could possibly need. We may feel comfortable, safe, independent, and entertained, but also, we feel completely sad.

I get it. Everyone does it. But this thing that everyone does is just not working for anyone. Research says that more than "three in five Americans report being chronically lonely," and that number is "on the rise," stats that are costly and grave.[1] Anxiety, depression, suicidal thoughts are all on the rise.

Is this living? Is this how life is supposed to go?

Before we get into all of it, let me skip to the answer. NO. IT ISN'T SUPPOSED TO BE THIS WAY!

There is a way to live life less alone. There is. It costs something, sometimes more than most are willing to pay. But it's worth it; it's doable; it's possible. Stick with me.

It is possible to live life connected—intimately connected—to other people. And no, we're not going to spend the next seven weeks figuring out how to build a new group of best friends.

---

1 Elena Renken, "Most Americans Are Lonely, and Our Workplace Culture May Not Be Helping," *NPR News*, January 3, 2020, https://www.npr.org/sections/health-shots/2020/01/23/798676465/most-americans-are-lonely-and-our-workplace-culture-may-not-be-helping.

Here is what we are going to do:

▷ We are going to look back at how almost every generation has lived until us—and how we are living differently.

▷ We are going to talk about community and all the ways it can be in our lives that maybe you've never thought of.

▷ We are going to look at what God meant relationships to be and how we have hijacked that.

▷ We are going to dream of a new way to find our people and to do life with them in more intentional ways.

My dream for you, God's plan for you, is to build a culture of community in every part of your life.

ON PURPOSE

Why do we expect close friends to somehow appear in our busy lives? We think our acquaintances should just magically produce our few best friends. *Then* our relational needs will be met. Back in the day, people found their friends from their larger village of interconnected people. Think village life, small-town life, or agrarian life, or tribes.

People's needs were met because of the way they lived: close. But because we see community as an accessory, not the essential fabric of life as our ancestors did by default, we are lonely. We are looking to plug a gaping hole. The hole is bigger than a couple people could ever fill, and so we live constantly disappointed, and we further isolate ourselves. It's time to break that cycle—on purpose.

THE BIG PICTURE

We'd all love to make a few new friends. But I have a bigger vision for you. God has a bigger vision for you.

I want us to trade lonely and isolated lives that experience brief bursts of connectedness for intimately connected lives that know only brief bursts of feeling alone.

Think I'm crazy? I'm here to tell you I'm not. I've experienced what I'm fighting for. I have observed with my own two eyes. And once you see it, you can't unsee it. You can't *not* fight for this kind of life.

But most everything in your life flies in the face of what I am about to invite you to do along our journey together. Specifically:

> Your routines.

> The way that you buy groceries.

> Your housing situation.

> Whether or not you live near your family.

> The church you choose to be part of.

> What you do this weekend.

> And deeper still: How open you choose to be about your sufferings. Your anxiety. Your pain.

▷ And whether you'll ask the hard question of the person you love who is drinking too much.

▷ And if you'll forgive and fight for the people who have hurt you deeper than you could ever imagine.

It's a risk. It's all a risk to go deeper into this with me. But if you feel that ache for connection, you're in the right place.

STUDY ::

Work through these pages as your
Introduction to God's Plan for Community.

WHAT IS COMMUNITY AND WHERE DID IT COME FROM?

IN THE BEGINNING, GOD

When we look back in Scripture, we see how intentionally God designed us for and invites us to community. In fact, He *is* community.

God existed in relationship with Himself before any of us were here. It's called the Trinity. God is one, and God is three. (If this feels confusing, don't worry. It hurts my brain still, and I've been to seminary.)

The key point is this: **For all of eternity, God has existed in relationship—as Father, Spirit, and Son (Jesus).**

About the **Father and Son**, we learn in Colossians 1:15–17:

"The Son is the image of the invisible God, the firstborn over all creation. For in him all things were created: things in heaven and on earth, visible and invisible, whether thrones or powers or rulers or authorities; all things have been created through him and for him. He is before all things, and in him all things hold together."

And Jesus tells us about the **Spirit** in relation to both of them in John 16:13–15:

"he will guide you into all the truth. He will not speak on his own; he will speak only what he hears, and he will tell you what is yet to come. He will glorify me because it is from me that he will receive what he will make known to you. All that belongs to the Father is mine. That is why I said the Spirit will receive from me what he will make known to you."

Scripture says that the Son exists to glorify the Father, and that the Father exists to glorify the Son. It says that the Spirit exists to glorify them both. What that means is: they help each other, they promote each other, they serve each other, and they love each other. What's more, this exchange has been going on for all of eternity.

Our God created us *out of* relationship *for* relationship—and not relationship that is surface level, or self-seeking. No, the relationship He has in mind for us is

      sacrificial,

          intimate,

               moment-by-moment connection.

Beautiful.

Relational. It's who we are, because it's who God is.

NEXT, FAMILY

First, God existed in community. Then we were created to join in that relationship.

We weren't just created *for* community, **we were created because of it.** We aren't craving something good for us, like vegetables or vitamins; we are craving the fundamental reason we were created: relationship.

Genesis 1:27–28 tells us:

"So God created mankind in his own image, in the image of God he created them; male and female he created them."

"God blessed them and said to them, 'Be fruitful and increase in number; fill the earth and subdue it. Rule over the fish in the sea and the birds in the sky and over every living creature that moves on the ground.'"

God's first community on earth is a family, a community "in his own image." Verse 31 says he called it "very good." The only "not good" thing in the creation account was the fact that Adam was first by himself:

"The LORD God said, "It is not good for the man to be alone. I will make a helper suitable for him." (Genesis 2:18)

And so God created Eve and gave she and Adam everything they needed in order to thrive on the earth.

They were naked, and unashamed (Genesis 2:25). No shame before each other, and no shame before God. Just free, beautiful love and the safety of authentic relationship. They shared the goal of caring for creation. They were given a boundary (just one) around the tree of the knowledge of good and evil (vv. 16–17). And they had all the time in the world to enjoy God, His creation, and each other.

Thriving, fruitful community was God's original plan for humankind.

FINALLY, THERE'S HEAVEN

I like to think of Eden as a little bit of heaven on earth. In this brief moment in time, before sin entered, Adam and Eve were functioning perfectly as a microcosm of community. So, we're going to look at what was going on there and discover how we can do it too. As Jesus taught us to pray, this is what we desire:

"Your kingdom come, your will be done, on earth as it is in heaven,". (Matthew 6:10)

We are going to seek His will, on earth as it is in heaven. So what made Eden heaven on earth? What can we do to see for ourselves Jesus' vision, "On earth as it is in heaven"?

We'll discover five ways.

FIRE — Goal: Proximity / Barrier: Busyness

OPEN DOORS — Goal: Transparency / Barrier: Pain/Shame

ANVIL — Goal: Accountability / Barrier: Pride

SHOVEL — Goal: Shared Purpose / Barrier: Shallow/Small Talk

TABLE — Goal: Consistency / Barrier: Conflict

FIVE TASTES OF HEAVEN

Here's what we're going to work to reclaim together in this study. Five particular things characterized the healthy, balanced vision of community in Eden. They were:

1. **Proximity**: Adam and Eve were with each other all the time, and they walked with God closely. (Genesis 3:8)

2. **Transparency**: They were fully known and fully loved—naked and unashamed. (Genesis 2:25)

3. **Accountability**: God set boundaries for them around the Tree, and they were accountable to Him for keeping them. (Genesis 2:17)

4. **Purpose**: They shared a job, caring for God's beautiful creation. (Genesis 2:15)

5. **Consistency**: They woke up and showed up every day, with all the time in the world to pour into each other—originally made to flourish without the brokenness of sin and death and conflict.

These five "tastes of heaven" are our framework. God gave us a model to follow here. **God established a perfect community that we can work to reclaim here and now.** These five things will be our goals in our time together. And we'll talk about what keeps us from them—and how we can fight together to get them back.

In this study we're going to build, step by step, a reality out of God's vision for community. That may sound huge and intimidating, but it's really made of small shifts and changes. And eventually you wake up and those small things

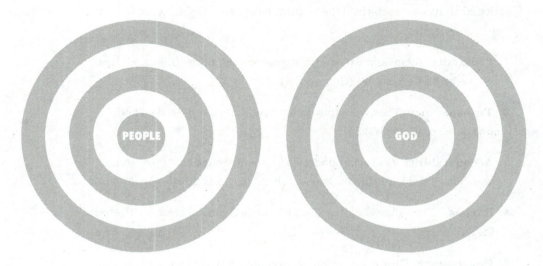

have made something beautiful. In the projects at the end of each session, I invite you to peel back the layers of your own experiences with friendship, community, and what you believe about God. This week, we'll do two short projects as a group to prime our hearts and minds to continue on this journey together.

Take a few minutes to reflect by yourself. How close do you feel to people right now? How close do you feel to God/Jesus? Put a dot where you are on each bullseye.

> **Farther out/way outside the circle:** *Feeling basic lack of human contact/deep divides between you and others.*

> **A little farther in:** *Wading around, but it doesn't get as deep as you'd like.*

> **Approaching the center:** *Some good times, but often overwhelmed by experiencing hurt, conflict, humanity that is making you question the need for community or how much you want to give.*

> **Smack in the center:** *You've had a taste (or you've got a great community), but want to pull other people in. You'd like to see God's will come through community, for the healing of the world.*

We were built for God. And until we come to Him as our Father and friend, we will keep looking to people to fill what only God can. And yes, that relationship is first, but that relationship is meant to send us into loving others.

If you put God in His right place in your heart, you will more likely put people in theirs.

Charles Spurgeon wrote, "We shall not long have love for man if we do not first and chiefly cultivate love for God."

Because you've shown up for this study, I know you're brave enough to take a real look at this issue and not run away, pretending everything's fine. So, begin by taking a moment to reflect on and/or share your answer to these questions:

▶ *Why is this so hard for you?*

▶ *What are your hopes and expectations of these weeks together?*

CONCLUSION

HOW WE WERE BUILT TO LIVE

The great thing about it is, this isn't just about us feeling better right now. It's about forever—for everyone. It's God's plan to reach his people—essentially, to save the world. Big stuff. But it starts small.

Do you believe that true, radical connection is what you were built for? Does this sound possible? Read each of the following bullets into the middle of this sentence and think about your answers.

Do . . .

▷ long conversations with people who have known you for years

▷ people who drop by with food unannounced

▷ regular unscheduled and unhurried meet-ups with people who feel like family

▷ people who show up early to help you cook and stay late to clean up

▷ people who hurt you and who you hurt (but you work through it instead of quitting each other)

▷ people to live on mission, who challenge you and make you better

▷ people who are your people, and you are theirs

. . . seem impossible?

It's possible. All of it.

SEE ::

Watch Video Session 1 now.

Use streaming code on inside cover or DVD.

THE DISRUPTION OF COMMUNITY

WHAT HAPPENED TO GOD'S ORIGINAL PLAN?

I think it was sometime in 2014 when the thought occurred to me that I didn't have any friends. I should clarify: I had plenty of friends, but those friends and I all had very full lives, which meant that our interactions were erratic—and rare. Back then, I was traveling a lot speaking and doing ministry, and while being on the road provided plenty of life-giving interactions with other women, reentry at home often came with a sting. Did any of my "friends" even realize I'd been gone?

This wasn't my friends' fault, of course. They had lives of their own. In fact, they likely were asking the same questions of me: "Does Jennie even know what is going on in my life? Does she even care?"

Isn't this familiar? **We all are just kind of waiting.** Waiting for connection to find us. We are waiting for someone else to initiate. Someone else to be there for us. Someone else to make the plans or ask the questions.

My friend and neuro-relational expert Curt Thompson says it this way, "Every newborn comes into this world looking for someone looking for her." And that never quits being true.

You and I are both a little needy.

God built us this way, in fact.

And yet it's hard to need people. No, it's *terrifying* to need people, because sometimes when we do, it feels like they're not there.

THE "MIDDLE OF THE CRY" FRIEND

I have a friend, Lindsey, who calls me in the **middle** of her good cry, when she's hurting, raw, confused about why she is even so sad. **She lets me into the mess of that moment because she knows that suffering alone will only make the suffering worse.** When I cry, I get it all out of my system and then maybe call a friend the next day. Because I hate how needy I actually am. **I am embarrassed in my brokenness, and I wonder if anyone would really want to be in the middle of that good cry with me.**

Which is ironic, because I love when Lindsey calls me crying. It makes me feel needed, and who doesn't want someone to need them? So why do we keep trying to pretend that our need isn't real?

I think it's because it's messy.

We've replaced intrusive, real conversations with small talk and soul-bearing, deep, connected living with supper clubs and book clubs—because the superficial stuff is less messy. But lonely or deeply connected life is messy. Jesus knew it.

"In this world you will have trouble," He said in John 16:33.

We were never meant to do the mess of trouble here alone—sobbing our way through, alone on a bathroom floor. The magic of the best of relationships *is the mess*, the sitting-on-the-floors-of-bathrooms-together, hugging-and-sobbing mess.

Hiding my neediness is actually a painful topic for me. It always has been.

I've hurt people.

They've hurt me.

I have failed relationships with people I know I have hurt. Some have forgiven me, and some have walked away. I am certain that if they knew I was doing a study about friendship, some would shake their heads and roll their eyes.

They'd be right. As I say, I'm better than I used to be, but I'm far from perfect here. And yet I'm going to keep at it. Why? Because the more I look into the why of our neediness and the problem of our loneliness, the more convinced I am that at our core, we are made to be fully known and fully loved. Loved and known regularly and over time by people in our day-in, day-out lives, not just once in a while in the presence of a paid therapist.

HOW DID THINGS GET SO BROKEN?

I am betting I'm not the only one who doesn't like to bring my mess. Who prefers to isolate and hide. Apparently, it's what people have been doing from the very beginning of time.

This week we'll read about Adam and Eve, how they got themselves in a mess, and how they hid. Sin brought shame into the world. And you and me? We deal with the same thing every day, in our own ways.

Their enemy *hated* their thriving in that Garden. He slithered in and started his sabotage. And He hates our thriving today, so He uses the same old tricks to try to break down what God built.

Those fig leaves are still our go-to today, self-protecting rather than moving toward people in our hurt, covering our mess with a "doing fine here!" We are hurt, and therefore, we hurt. And the enemy calls it a good day's work. Because our attempts to cover shame will never be sufficient—we'll always keep running and hiding and spinning.

But there's good news here. God doesn't leave us this way. This is *not good* for His precious creation. He won't stand for it. He comes to rescue us.

STUDY ::

Read Genesis 3

One of the most important tools you can possibly possess is the ability to sit down with only your Bible, pen and paper, and discover truth for yourself. I love creating tools to aid in that, but ultimately, I want you to be building this muscle as we journey together. So, before we go any further, we're going to focus on what I call the three keys to effective personal Bible study:

Observation

Interpretation

Application

Throughout this journey, I am going to give you the opportunity to practice each of these. I use them in each of my studies, because it's so important to build confidence in you to practice these skills in your own time of Bible study.

Before we dive too deep into chapter 3, do you remember this verse from Genesis 2?

"Then the LORD God said, 'It is not good that the man should be alone; I will make him a helper fit for him'". (Genesis 2:18)

Connection was God's original vision—connection with God and connection with each other, and God in the center. But the enemy *hates* connection. His strategic plan was to divide humans from God and humans from each other.

▷ *In Genesis 3:1–5, write out the lies the enemy uses to convince Eve to eat the fruit.*

▷ *What was his goal?*

▷ *What was Adam and Eve's plan to handle the broken relationship they now had with their creator? (vv. 7–10)*

▷ *What did they feel?*

▷ *In verses 8–13, write out the questions God asks Adam and Eve.*

▷ *What was His goal?*

Because God is just and because sin naturally has consequences, let's look at what the consequences for humanity became after Adam and Eve rejected God and His plan:

For the woman (v. 16)

For the man (vv. 17–19)

For the enemy (vv. 14–16)

Hint: The one to crush the enemy's head would be Jesus. (2 Corinthians 2:15)

Even in the midst of God's justice, there was a promise of mercy. That mercy would come in the form of a person, His Son Jesus. Knowing all that it would cost Him and knowing how broken humanity would be, life through Adam and Eve continues and is promised.

▷ *In verses 20-21, what does God promise Adam and Eve?*

THERE'S A REASON FOR THIS

If you are still thinking that loneliness is just your problem, and that something is specifically wrong with you as an individual, maybe it's a relief to think about the fact that there are reasons for this. Big reasons that aren't due to your personal failings.

▷ **There are sin reasons**. As we just covered, humans are prone to this.

▷ **There are historical reasons, too.** Modern life has brought a breakdown of the village structure, and our conveniences and technologies allow us to hide and be independent in ways never experienced before. American society is literally built to celebrate independence. It's pumped into us from childhood. But as good as it is to be "independent," there's another side to that coin. It can go too far.

▷ **There is an enemy** who is doing this to you on purpose, and who wants you to think something is wrong with you, *so* you'll continue to isolate.

There is no greater weapon the enemy uses to destroy our connection with each other and with God than **shame**. Shame is so effective because it accomplishes so much with one dark feeling. Just like Adam and Eve,

We hide from God and each other.

We try to cover it up and pretend we're okay.

And we try to justify why we just did all of that.

All we want is to be okay with God, ourselves, and the people we love. But something went wrong.

Satan. A choice. An apple. Shame. Immediate shame.

But of course, God found them.

God wanted them to come out of sin and hiding and shame and come back into relationship with Him. But God is just and righteous, and if He were to tolerate sin with no punishment, then He would be abiding that sin. Sin required payment, and the price was death. But he promised Adam and Eve in Genesis exactly what would come, which was the blood sacrifice of an animal. He covered them with clothes made from that skin. It was a picture of the gospel, that one day a blood sacrifice would be made to cover our sins once and for all.

This remains God's desire—that we would be in right relationship with Him. This is the story of God. He has *fought* for us to be right with Him. He loves us so much that even when we turn away from Him, He fights to get us back. He values us so much, and He has set us in our places and created us for connection and purposes that are beyond what we can imagine.

He did all of that because He is good.

He is so loving and powerful, and He wants to share Himself with us. And if all this is true, then we need never be in bondage to shame again. We have been made beautifully and totally free.

"If the Son sets you free, you will be free indeed". (John 8:36)

The reason the gospel changes everything is it's the only antidote on planet earth that eradicates shame. But we don't believe it—because how could we truly be forgiven and reconciled to a perfect God when we know deep down we're so jacked up?

We were dead, separated, and helpless (naked and ashamed), but:

"because of his great love for us, God, who is rich in mercy made us alive with Christ even when we were dead in our transgressions". (Ephesians 2:4-5)

We live under this curse until we die—in our relationships with others, with ourselves, and with our God, unless the gospel changes everything about who we are and how we relate to our God and each other.

▷ *How has the gospel changed your relationship with shame?*

▷ *How has the gospel freed you from shaming others?*

You can never be at peace with other people disappointing you and with other people's sin until you realize you need that grace that the gospel promised as much as they do.

Come Out of Hiding

"There is no one righteous, not even one; there is no one who understands; there is no one who seeks God. All have turned away". (Romans 3:10–12)

This is the story of humankind. And you see the repercussions of that independence and division everywhere. But nowhere is it clearer than in our relationships. **Nothing hurts more, nothing steals our thoughts, nothing disrupts our happiness more than difficult or broken relationships with the people who were supposed to be there for us.**

But we all hurt. We all sin. We all push away. We all are guilty.

Nothing in my relational life has helped me more than coming to terms with these simple truths:

You will disappoint me. I will disappoint you. God will never disappoint us.

It shifts all the expectations from people to God, and God is excellent at handling our deepest desires.

Even after you find your people, those relationships will never be all you hope and dream them to be. Your people will be more hurtful, more sinful, and more disappointing than you wish. But guess what? You'll be these things too!

Hurting people hurt.

But equally true is that only forgiven people can truly forgive.

It's why I love the gospel. It is the only story in the world where God rescues us from hiding. He restores us and tells us that "there is now no more condemnation for those who are in Christ Jesus" (Romans 8:1). And because we are restored and have full access to our God again—a God who forgives—we have the tools to change the cycle of hiding.

WHO ARE YOU, LORD? & WHAT DO YOU WANT FROM ME?

Read Ephesians 2:1-10. In light of what you read, answer the questions above.

PROJECT 1
REFLECT

▷ *How would you really describe God right now? Not the Bible study answers.*

▷ *Do you feel close to God right now? Y/N*

▷ *How are these words causing you to feel close?*

PROJECT 2
CONNECT

▷ *Take a blanket outside, play a worship song, and have a conversation with God.*

▷ *Write about that experience. Here are four questions to ask God while you're on the blanket:*

▸ What is holding me back from being close to You?

▸ What am I not believing about You that's true?

▸ What's holding me back from being close to community?

▸ What am I not believing about having deep community that is true?

PROJECT 3
CONSIDER

▷ *What has been your deepest hurt in a friendship experience? How has that birthed a fear in you?*

▷ *Bravely think back on times you've been rejected by others. What fears or resolutions did those experiences plant in you?*

▷ *Now identify your greatest:*

▸ Friendship fears:

▸ Friendship rejections:

▸ Bad friendship experiences:

(This is depressing, but I promise we'll use these for good.)

PROJECT 4
ACCESS

▷ *Look back to yesterday, when you thought of the ways you saw close community working in those five tastes of heaven. When was the one time you felt the MOST connected to community? (ex., camp, neighborhood, college, sports team, family reunions, etc.)*

▷ *What were the COMPONENTS that made that community possible? (ex., shared mission, proximity, outward focus, etc.)*

▶ How much physical time did you spend together?

▶ How did you have fun together?

▶ Did you ever work through conflict together? What was hard? What was easy?

▶ Did you have a shared purpose, and what was it?

▶ How well did you know each other?

▶ What kind of things did you talk about?

CONCLUSION

NO CONDEMNATION

Let me tell you the greatest way to fight shame:

1. Live aware of your weakness and sin.

2. Live aware of the endless grace of our God that covers it all.

When you are fully in touch with how weak you are and how much of a sinner you are, as well as fully in touch with the power of God to make sinners right and the grace of God to cover those sins, that is a free person. That is a person no longer bound by shame. That is a person who can dangerously go live out the calling and the mission of God in her life. Those are my favorite people to be with, too. I can say anything to them without fear, because they know there is no condemnation—they're in touch with their own sins, and they are going to give back to me the love of God. May we be those people, too. And may we disciple and make those people on earth. That is how the world changes: people truly free of shame. They are rare, they're amazing, they look and live totally differently—and they're contagious.

People like this are the ones who have called me out of hiding. If I'm a chronic fig-leaf wearer, pretending to be totally fine, some of these miraculous free people have extended their hands to me and invited me into a new life. But it took a choice to stop hiding. My small group, for instance, has started to crack me open like a nut—to be that village that doesn't quit and never goes away. At first, it was off-putting and uncomfortable. But then I realized, it was life to me. We're going to talk about building this kind of community in the coming weeks. But the first step in that process is realizing you're not alone, and it's okay to come out of hiding.

SEE ::

Watch Video Session 2 now.
Use streaming code on inside cover or DVD.

PROXIMITY

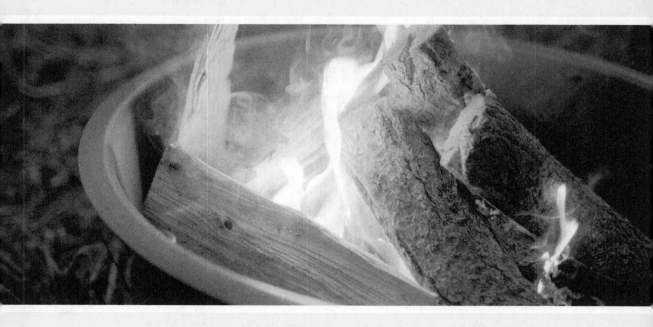

GOD'S PRESENCE

Since the Stone Age, we humans have been building fires. There are plenty of practical reasons for this: cooking food, forging metal, staving off a bitterly cold winter, or simple coziness. We can get lost in a trance, looking at flames. Given that we spend most of our day strategizing and planning and working and following through, finally comes a real pull to sit down, relax, calm the mind, and chat. A fire gives us all these things. "Gathering around an evening fire is an important opportunity for calm information exchange," writes Christopher Lynn, associate professor of anthropology at the University of Alabama. "During the day, biological rhythms produced by elevated cortisol and other stress hormones keep humans awake and provide the pre-coffee bump needed to be motivated to get things done. But as those levels drop in the evening, we are able to sit and relax. We're in a mood to tell and listen to stories."

I remember reading of an anthropologist who spent nearly two hundred days living with the bushmen of Botswana one time and discovered that while about three-fourths of the tribe's daytime conversations centered on work-related talk, more than three-fourths of their nighttime conversations—always held around a fire, incidentally—centered on spirituality or what the researcher called "enthralling stories." The tribesmen talked about adventures they'd had. And about elephants they'd encountered. And about politics, and about religion, and about the dreams they had for their lives.

Throughout history, villages come together around fires to cook, to plan, to dance and sing, to be together after the kids are in bed. Yep. **Fire has been the communal spot since the beginning of time.**

Fires bring us together . . . real life, face to face, no phones, together.

I think we crave something like this in our busy lives. We're all rushing around, faces down in our phones, or going from one thing to the next being busy, and we don't ever get to that point where we sit down with our neighbors at the end of the day and talk. Where we stare into the flames and share life. In fact, a lot of us don't really know the people around us— much less are we on "fireside-chat" terms. I know I've found myself with the realization that I would have to drive 45 minutes each way to get to someone I could really talk to.

Who are these people who live around us?

Hopefully we're all peeping out of our hiding places now. Out of our isolation. But for a lot of us, busyness has become a place where we hide from the others in our path. Our heads are down, we're rushing from place to place, and we don't see folks around us. Our real, legitimate, good things like working and staying healthy, keeping a family going and keeping children alive, doing all the many, many things we do takes a *lot* of time. And at the prospect of adding one more thing to it—even if that's making an effort to find friends nearby—we just deflate. I get it. It feels like one thing too many.

The good thing is, community isn't designed to be "another thing on top" of everything else. It will never work that way. It's made to weave within, all throughout, the good things we're doing with our lives—right here, right now—making us stronger and making things better through and through. From the beginning of the day until its end, around the fire. And it starts with bringing people into our right-now lives. Into our right-here. Opening up to those we're in proximity to.

But a lot of us are strangers with the people we bump into day to day. It feels weird.

It's *supposed* to make us feel tortured inside when we act "alone" in the context of perfectly good people we could be hanging out with and loving well.

And yet far too many of us have adopted this as a lifestyle. We go through life barely noticing the people God has put right in our path, insisting that we're all alone in the world and that nobody cares. **The truth is this: We are meant to be emotionally close to the people we are physically close to.**

Proximity is that first taste of heaven we're going to talk about—the first attribute of God-designed community that we want to reclaim today. God is coming to find us and bring us back into a *together* way of life. We've overburdened ourselves, but God is coming to relieve us. We've isolated, but He wants His kids back. He's going to pull us out of our hiding places and out of our busy. Into a village. Into proximity with Him, and with others.

So how do we recreate a sense of real proximity, living WITH the people who are physically, geographically close to us? We learn to dwell where we are. And to do that, we look to the first Dweller. He is the inventor of proximity, and Dwelling is his MO.

STUDY ::

Read Genesis 3:8

Dwelling with us has been the heart of God since creation. With God. With each other. Is the vision. God is in the center of it, and we are together with him. He shows us this throughout Scripture.

1. HE DWELLED IN THE GARDEN.

Even though this was after they sinned, the implication is that God regularly visited with Adam and Eve.

▷ *What was God's desire for Adam and Eve?*

2. HE DWELLED IN THE TABERNACLE.

Read Exodus 25:8–9.

Write out the details of God's desires.

▷ *What was the purpose of the tabernacle?*

3. HE DWELLED IN HIS PROMISES.

God used His prophets to deliver a promise of a time that we would be reconciled forever to Him. Permanent dwelling.

Read Jeremiah 31:31–34.

▷ *What were God's desires and promise of reconciliation?*

4. HE DWELLED AMONG US, IN PERSON, THROUGH CHRIST.

Then finally a baby would come, the seed that was promised in Genesis.

Read Matthew 1:22–23.

▷ *What were God's desires through Christ?*

5. HE DWELLS INSIDE US EVEN NOW.

God gave us the Holy Spirit to live within us.

Read 1 Corinthians 3:16.

▷ *For those who trust Immanuel, what does God promise?*

6. HE DWELLS IN THE CHURCH.

Then He promises to dwell in His church gathered on earth.

Read Ephesians 2:22

▷ *How are we being built?*

God can feel far off, but what hope do these verses give us for our proximity to God?

▷ *Describe the hope given in each verse or passage.*

    ▶ Genesis 3:8

    ▶ Exodus 25:8–9

    ▶ Jeremiah 31:31–34

    ▶ Matthew 1:22–23

    ▶ 1 Corinthians 3:16

    ▶ Ephesians 2:22

▷ *How have you felt God dwelling with you in your life?*

▷ *In what ways/situations is it hard for you to believe that God is dwelling with you?*

PUT IN OUR DWELLING PLACES

Proximity with God and with each other. That's what equips us to combat the enemy of busyness.

Acts 17:26–27 says,

> "God made from one man every nation of mankind to live on all the face of the earth, having determined allotted periods and the boundaries of their dwelling place, that they should seek God, and perhaps feel their way toward him and find him."

How beautiful is that? God set you in your place and time to LOVE people to seek Him and find Him.

▷ *Look up right now. Since you are alive on the face of the earth, what is your dwelling place? What are the allotted periods and boundaries of that dwelling place?*

> *Do you believe God put them there?*

> *Has busyness kept you from looking closely at these places?*

In these boundaries and in these places, we find our people, and together we build safe, beautiful outposts that offer the love of God.

As if that wasn't enough of a reason to love Jesus! He made a way for us toward God and toward each other. But He went one step further: He modeled how Proximity would look. **He chose to come to earth not only to die for our sins but to show us how to live as children of God. Together.**

So here are just a few things you need to know about when God came to earth:

> Jesus was born into an earthly family, with a mom and a dad and siblings.

> He grew up in a neighborhood with family friends and other kids.

> He learned a trade—carpentry—from his earthly dad and spent most of His earthly life building physically useful things.He experienced temptation but never sinned.

> He laughed and learned and sang and grew up in the context of a village.

> He found his people in unexpected places, not universities or temples. They were often considered to be the wrong ethnicities, the wrong gender, the wrong age, the wrong status, the wrong personality type, the wrong people by any onlooker's estimation.

Jesus' people were all wrong, except that they were willing. And they were wanting. And they were all in.

That, by the way, seems to be the only universally clear marker of the small group of people Jesus chose to spend His time with. They were willing. They were wanting. They were ALL IN. These people: He was in proximity to them, and He opened His heart to them and made them His village.

On another level, the Bible shows Him pushing the crowds away and choosing twelve. Within that twelve, there were three He spent the most time with. They were His closest people. The ones He confided in the most. The short version? **It's okay to be selective as we go forward.** You will need to be.

Jesus and His people would go on to help a lot of people "feel their way" toward God. What began in a village morphed into a tight group of people, who would reach generations and the ends of the earth. This matters. This end-game matters to God.

JESUS INITIATED

We get enough of Jesus' life in the gospels to know that Jesus was an incredible initiator. He noticed people. He stopped for a conversation. He even invited himself over to Zacchaeus' house for dinner.

"He entered Jericho and was passing through. And behold, there was a man named Zacchaeus. He was a chief tax collector and was rich. And he was seeking to see who Jesus was, but on account of the crowd he could not, because he was small in stature. So he ran on ahead and climbed up into a sycamore tree to see him, for he was about to pass that way. And when Jesus came to the place, he looked up and said to him, 'Zacchaeus, hurry and come down, for I must stay at your house today.' So he hurried and came down and received him joyfully. . . . And Jesus said to him, 'Today salvation has come to this house, since he also is a son of Abraham. For the Son of Man came to seek and to save the lost'". (Luke 19:1–10)

Imagine inviting yourself to someone's house. The nerve! And yet, how great! Jesus was always seeking people out where they were. And it was a small geographical area. I have been blessed to be able to do some work in Israel, and the thing that surprised me more than any other is the radius where most of Jesus' life took place. Israel is a small country, roughly the size of

New Jersey. If He did all He did within just a few square miles, imagine what kinds of connections are waiting for us in the Google Maps circle around our house. What's stopping us?

Truth is, the enemy wants to shut you down, make you afraid to initiate, cause you to not prioritize the people right in front of you. He wants us to live surrounded by people but never deeply connecting to them, so we don't change, we don't grow, we don't even fully live. We mostly end up stuck in self-pity about how we don't have any friends when dozens of people in front of us could fit the bill, and certainly could use someone reaching out to them.

Friendship should in its truest form reflect aspects of who God is and how He loves. Which brings me to a question: Who has God put in your life—here and now and right under your nose—who you haven't appreciated yet?

WHO ARE YOU, LORD? & WHAT DO YOU WANT FROM ME?

Read Philippians 2:1-11. In light of what you read, answer the questions above.

PROJECT 1
IMAGINE

▶ *Who is your village?*

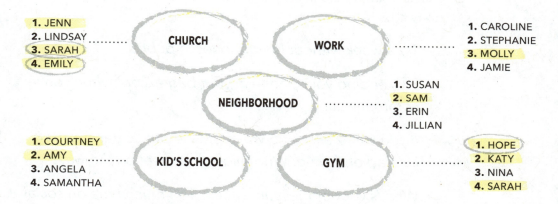

1. JENN
2. LINDSAY
3. SARAH
4. EMILY

CHURCH

WORK

1. CAROLINE
2. STEPHANIE
3. MOLLY
4. JAMIE

NEIGHBORHOOD

1. SUSAN
2. SAM
3. ERIN
4. JILLIAN

1. COURTNEY
2. AMY
3. ANGELA
4. SAMANTHA

KID'S SCHOOL

GYM

1. HOPE
2. KATY
3. NINA
4. SARAH

▶ *Who are the people already in your life and the places you're already frequenting? Who could you connect with in a deeper way?*

PROJECT 2
UNPLUG

Busyness is the enemy of Proximity. We are simply too rushed to look at who is around us. Pinpoint where you tend to be the busiest and install some safety nets.

▷ *Try a week without headphones in public.*

▷ *Try keeping your phone in your bag except when you're communicating.*

▷ *If you can, walk somewhere or take public transport instead of driving. Who might you meet on the way?*

▷ *What's your biggest time suck? Too much time on social media? Address it directly for a week. Some ideas:*

   ▸ Install a limiter.

   ▸ Every time you feel the impulse, reach out to someone or thank someone or simply thank God for someone and pray for their well-being.

   ▸ Write someone an actual note when the urge strikes.

▷ *Events crowding your schedule?*

   ▸ Is there something you can say no to this week that will open up some time for people?

PROJECT 3
RISK

▷ *Scroll through your phone and make a list of the people whose numbers you've saved. Who are these people?*

▷ *From that list, start a list of people you enjoy and want to spend more time with.*

▷ *Ask someone from that list to do something you're already doing (go on a walk, play date, coffee, pick vegetables from your garden, join your family dinner, etc.). Start clocking some time.*

Research shows that it takes "50 hours of interaction to move from acquaintance to casual friend, about 90 hours to move from casual friend to friend, and more than 200 hours to qualify as a best friend."

PROJECT 4
REFLECT

▶ *Think of people who have invested in your life recently. List their names here.*

▶ Why do you value that person and what have they done to show you they value you?

▶ *Write a text or a note to somebody you appreciate who has been a good friend to you.*

▶ How can you give to someone else on your new friend list the kind of friendship you've been blessed to receive?

CONCLUSION

LIGHT A FIRE

During the Covid quarantine of 2020, Zac and I often took walks around the neighborhood, and one of my favorite sights was a front yard stuffed with six cheap plastic Adirondack chairs, all placed in a ring. On one of the chairs was always perched a bottle of mosquito spray, as if to say, "Pandemic, quarantine, not even mosquitos are gonna keep us from getting together!" In the middle of those rings of chairs, I often saw a fire pit. There we are, gathering around the fire again. Presence. Proximity. Dwelling.

So, why not literally get a fire pit? Put it in your front yard if you have one. We got one that we keep in the front with an inviting blaze, and we always have stuff for s'mores and drinks at the ready. Even if that's not an option for you, think about a good gathering place for you. Maybe it's your favorite café. Or a pub terrace. Then **you invite.** You spontaneously and regularly start inviting people in your everyday world. And people will say no, and you keep inviting anyway. **And then you ask real questions,** the kind that makes everyone just uncomfortable enough that you might actually get to know them, and you go first and answer, and you sit and stay and laugh. Bring the fire back. Jesus sat with His people around a fire, and—even if ours is a metaphorical one— we can do the same. We dwell. We live in proximity.

This is possible. And you aren't the only one craving it. **Everyone is!**

SEE ::

Watch Video Session 3 now.
Use streaming code on inside cover or DVD.

SESSION 4

TRANSPARENCY

Walls are a luxury, a privilege. I learned this in Haiti while standing on the hill that overlooks tent city, which is only a two-hour flight from the coast of an affluent part of Florida. Blue tarps flapped in the wind, sheltering thousands of souls who were still displaced years after the earthquake. **How were they surviving without walls?**

Or how about Africa? I've visited dozens of African huts, and guess how many of them have permanent walls, let alone doors with locks? Zero. Beyond the lack of physical privacy, vulnerability and transparency are an intentional part of village life. They've got their hands full just trying to survive the rigors of daily life. They don't have room to hold pain and shut others out. They don't have the luxury of a closed, locked door . . . of tall, thick walls . . . of staying alone. **They need each other, and they know it.**

Same for us—we need each other, only most of us don't know it. Or prefer not to think about it.

While it's true that those people living in tough spots all over the world don't choose vulnerability as much as vulnerability chooses them, it's also true that vulnerability is choosing you and me too. **It's asking us to come out of our hiding and engage. To quit living behind our walls.**

While it's painful . . . excruciating, even, depending on the day . . . I'm learning that **vulnerability is the soil for intimacy, and that what waters intimacy is tears.** Real, raw, gut-wrenching honesty about what is happening inside your walls. Maybe that fight that made you want to leave your spouse last night. Or the addiction to pornography or sex that is eating you alive. Or the abortion you have never told anyone about. Or the small stuff that makes you cry—the anxieties and the aches inside.

I wish I could tell you it worked the other way. I wish I could tell you that a friendship built solely on laughter and good times would stand the test of time, would nourish the needs of your soul. I am good at all that stuff, you know?

But bear-your-soul intimacy? Not so much.

Whenever I hide behind my walls with the doors locked tight, I may be keeping out the potential of being misunderstood or wronged, devastated or disappointed, disillusioned or mistreated or hurt. But **I'm also keeping out the good things**—everything we are craving and built for: being encouraged, being held accountable, being seen, being loved, being known.

We must risk pain to have this kind of deep connection in our lives.

Transparency is the idea of living without walls. Where we can see what's really going on with each other. Where we gulp and take a deep breath and admit we need people. So, we're going to talk about how to reclaim that ability in our walled-off, locked-up world, where needing others is sometimes seen as weakness. I'm telling you—needing others isn't weak. It's a risk, yes, but it's one of the most satisfying things about being human. Knowing and being known, needing and being needed, is God's plan for us.

STUDY ::

Read Romans 8:1-4

▷ *Write out Romans 8:1 here:*

▷ *What does God promise in this verse?*

▷ *According to verse 2, what is the means of this kind of radical promise?*

▷ *What was the law powerless to do? (v. 3)*

▷ *What did Jesus do to make this kind of life possible? (v. 4)*

If you really believed these four verses, what would that mean in your life? How would it change your view of:

▷ *Yourself?*

▷ *Your sin?*

▷ *Your close relationships?*

▷ *Your ability to share your sin and struggles?*

THREE WALLS

Really, most of us have pretty good reasons for building walls. Maybe we've tried to be vulnerable and have been hurt or shamed. Maybe the people who were supposed to be our people ended up letting us down disastrously. Maybe we needed someone, and we were met with dismissal or derision or flat-out rejection, or we were taken advantage of and it really, deeply messed with us. That's legitimate pain. So we build walls of protection. That's my story, too. I opened up one too many times, and got hurt one too many times, and that's when I started pulling back.

Still, we can grow so lonely behind this wall. So what is God's answer to the Wall of Protection?

Wall of Protection vs. Armor of God

Read Ephesians 6:10–18

God doesn't leave us defenseless. We have power, and we have armor.

"Therefore put on the full armor of God, so that when the day of evil comes, you may be able to stand your ground, and after you have done everything, to stand. Stand firm then, with the belt of truth buckled around your waist, with the breastplate of righteousness in place, and with your feet fitted with the readiness that comes from the gospel of peace. In addition to all this, take up the shield of faith, with which you can extinguish all the flaming arrows of the evil one. Take the helmet of salvation and the sword of the Spirit, which is the word of God."

In his letter to the Ephesians, Paul isn't pretending that God doesn't care if we get hurt by flaming arrows. We have the Holy Spirit to give us discernment and lead us as we determine who to invite in, who to get close to. And if they do hurt us? It doesn't destroy us. We can risk hurt because God protects us from anything that would really take us out. Why hide behind a flimsy wall when we have this armor? **You don't have to pray power over the darkness, God says. I gave you power over the darkness. I am the power over the darkness . . . You have the Sword of the Spirit.**

WALL OF UNMET EXPECTATIONS VS. OUR HOPE

Read Hebrews 10:19–27

First let me say, it's good to have standards. To want good things from friends. Dependability. Trustworthiness. Kindness. Thoughtfulness. A great sense of humor. All wonderful things! But if we're not careful, we start making mental lists of all the things we want our friends to be for us, and if they miss the mark in some way, we draw back. We shield ourselves from disappointment over forgotten birthdays and unanswered texts and careless words. We put up the Wall of Unmet Expectations.

We dismantle this wall by placing our hope back where it belongs: in Jesus. We confess our hope in the only One who is forever faithful. Consider this from Hebrews 10:

"Let us draw near with a true heart in full assurance of faith, with our hearts sprinkled clean from an evil conscience and our bodies washed with pure water. Let us hold fast the confession of our hope without wavering, for he who promised is faithful. And let us consider how to stir up one another to love and good works, not neglecting to meet together, as is the habit of some, but encouraging one another, and all the more as you see the Day drawing near."

We can hold fast to our hope. We can be confident in Him, even if we're disappointed in people sometimes, and even if we ourselves disappoint. We stick with each other and try to make things right, because we have the ultimate Right who has sprinkled us fresh and clean.

WALL OF SHAME VS. THE TRUTH

Read Romans 8

Shame is something we'll come back to again and again in this study, because **one of the enemy's favorite lies is shame and because the cost of shame is connection.**

We wall ourselves off with shame when we want to avoid other people seeing us for who we are or provoking a deep shame already present in us.

You may be ashamed of being too needy, for mistakes in the past, things you are hiding, the way you "always" mess things up. Maybe **you don't share your struggles now because you've shared your struggles before, and "friends" punished you for being so real.**

The devil is good at his job. Shame is one of his favorite weapons to strip us of connection and community, and not only does shame leave us isolated, but shame also informs the thoughts we think as we sit there gravely alone.

"It's your fault that you are alone."

Ugh. Isn't it enough to be alone without feeling guilty over the fact that we are?

Isolation is one of shame's greatest goals. And, man, does it work!

We all experience this so often that we need a really dependable tool to combat it. This is how I see Romans 8. It's like a pick-axe I can pick up again and again to tear down the wall of shame.

"There is therefore now no condemnation for those who are in Christ Jesus. For the law of the Spirit of life has set you free in Christ Jesus from the law of sin and death. For God has done what the law, weakened by the flesh, could not do. By sending his own Son in the likeness of sinful flesh and for sin, he condemned sin in the flesh, in order that the righteous requirement of the law might be fulfilled in us, who walk not according to the flesh but according to the Spirit."

The new objective reality for those of you who believe in Jesus Christ and have trusted in Him as your Lord and Savior and put your hope in Him, is "there is therefore now no condemnation for those who are in Christ Jesus." This is your new reality. You don't have to feel shame. You can actually deal with it. It doesn't have to haunt you for the rest of your life. It doesn't have to define your decisions, your relationships, or your encounters with God.

However many times you have to repeat Romans 8:1 to yourself, however many times shame tries to snag you, it's a battle worth fighting and a wall worth tearing down. Because, really, the battle is already won. All we have to do is claim it.

WHO ARE YOU, LORD? & WHAT DO YOU WANT FROM ME?

Read Hebrews 10:24–25. In light of what you read, answer the questions above.

PROJECT 1
DISCOVER

You and I both are unhealthy people. (Hopefully not completely unhealthy, but somewhat unhealthy for sure.) Everyone has pockets of sin in their lives, and you and I are no different. The point? You will never find the perfect people to do life with, because those people don't exist. **You will always be doing community with sinners.** With that in mind, we approach this work with humility. A *lot* of humility. At the same time, we are told throughout Scripture to use discernment about the people we do life with.

In the "village" that Zac and I have built, there are two categories of people with whom I spend my time. Who is in these categories for you?

▷ *People who need me:*

▷ *People I need:*

We are called to love those who are not like us and who are not perfectly healthy good friends to us. This is one of the greatest callings of our lives.

But just like Jesus, we all need life-giving people who can serve as something of a safe place for us—**"our people,"** you might say.

▷ *Considering this, look back at the map of people in your life. Who are the most likely people for you to go deeper with? How would you place them on this graph?*

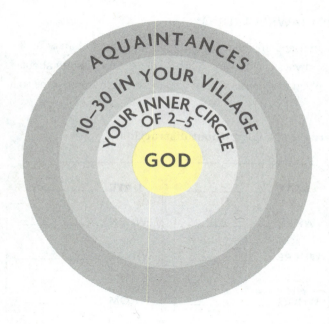

PROJECT 2
RISK

HOW TO GO FIRST (AWKWARDLY):

There is no way to take friendships deeper and to express need than to do it clumsily and it almost always is awkward. That's okay. Own it. Laugh about it. What I want to give you is a simple way to get started with friendships that appear safe.

1. Plan an uninterrupted time without distraction.

DATE _____	DATE _____	DATE _____
WHEN _____	WHEN _____	WHEN _____
WHERE _____	WHERE _____	WHERE _____
WITH WHOM _____	WITH WHOM _____	WITH WHOM _____

2. Prepare them in advance that it's going to be a deeper experience. Let them know: "I really want to share some things going on in my life right now." Or if it's a small group of people, "Can we talk about what's really going on in our lives tonight?"

3. **You lead the conversation.** Express why you want this to go deeper.

Share a difficulty in your life. Be as vulnerable as you can because **others will only be as deep and vulnerable as you are.**

Ask people the questions you wish they'd ask you:

> ▷ What feels hard for you right now?

> ▷ Where do you need help?

> ▷ What is making you happy right now?

> ▷ What is making you anxious?

Invite them in:

> ▷ Ask for advice.

> ▷ Ask for help.

> ▷ Tell them you like them! It's so rare that people actually hear the words: "Hey—I like spending time with you."

4. **Listening 101**

> ▷ Resist the temptation to solve.

> ▷ Repeat back what they said.

> ▷ No matter what, don't interrupt.

5. **Affirm each other** and express how much this meant to you.

6. **Plan a follow-up gathering**

PROJECT 3
ENGAGE

Fill out emotional mad libs, have your closest circle do the same, and share them together.

Emotional Mad Libs:

This week at work (or at home) I was busy with _____ and I felt _____ .

I think I felt that because _____ .

I wish that _____ would happen.

Very few people know that _____ is happening in my _____ .

I need _____ but I am afraid to ask for it.

I am afraid to open up because _____ .

The greatest way you could love me is to _____ .

PROJECT 4
HOPES VS. EXPECTATIONS

We talked above about the Wall of Expectations. Do any of these expectations of friends sound familiar to you?

> They will always be there when I want them to be.

> They will be great listeners.

> They will initiate.

> They will never misunderstand me.

> They will know how to comfort me.

> They will show up for me the way I show up for them.

> They will remember my birthday.

> They will encourage me.

> They will remember hard anniversaries in my life.

> They will never annoy me.

> They will know how often to communicate with me.

To expect deeper connection from people is not bad, but to try to get from people what only God can do for you will leave you constantly disappointed by friendships before you even start. Instead of the wall of expectations, start with one hope and communicate that regularly and often to the people you are trying to become better friends with.

When do you recall being disappointed by one of these things? Where do you feel let down most often?

Go back to each expectation and rephrase it as a hope you can communicate to someone in your inner circle. What would you kindly and vulnerably say to them?

CONCLUSION

CHOOSING TO NEED

I have something painful to share. A while back, one of my closest friends quit me. We'd been friends for more than a decade. The reason? I just didn't need her. She needed me, and I never seemed to need to her. So she said, "I can't do this anymore." And it was a shocking eye-opener for me. I had a transparency problem.

Recently I called her. We hadn't talked in a few years. I asked her if we could meet, and she replied yes. I was so nervous.

I wanted to apologize. I wanted to tell her I could now see what she saw. I wanted to try again and call each other friend again.

I sat across from her trembling and crying. She told me how I had hurt her and why she had pulled back. She told me things that were true, and I could understand how she had been so hurt. Still, I was guarded. She told me that she vividly remembered one time when I came over to her house and **cried** as I sat on her bed telling her my hurt. She said she'd never felt closer to me than she felt that day. But it was exhausting being in a friendship where she was the only needy one. My being a good friend to her was my needing her. I wanted, and still I want, to get better at this. I apologized. She apologized. We smiled.

I am so glad I braved opening the door again, a door I try to leave unlocked these days. People run through it more and more, and I still wince a little when they intrude and make me say all the hard and face all the hard. Still, I know that it's better this way. I am awkwardly learning. Together, transparent: it's **best** this way.

SEE ::

Watch Video Session 4 now.
Use streaming code on inside cover or DVD.

ACCOUNTABILITY

When I first moved from Austin to Dallas, I learned that my old camp counselor from twenty-five years prior happened to be living in the same town and attending the same church we'd chosen. I swallowed my embarrassment over being essentially friendless and asked if she'd be my friend. Yes, it was a little bit desperate. But I'm so glad I did.

As it turned out, she was in the process of joining a small group at our now-mutual church. "You know about the small groups?" she asked me under her breath, eyes doubtful.

"What about them?" I said, matching her reservation.

"*You join them for life,*" she said. Our church, as I would soon discover, takes community very, very seriously.

As in, tell-the-truth-about-your-struggles seriously.

As in, tell-the-*whole*-truth-about-your-struggles seriously.

As in, disclose-the-details-of-your-finances-with-each-other seriously.

Not kidding, even a little. In these community groups, *everything* is fair game.

So, she was giving me a little primer on our church's views on all of this, when she blurted out, "You and Zac should join ours!"

Uh. No.

"No, thank you." I mean, *Thank you!* And yet: *no.*

I wanted friends, but I also wanted some time to be sure that we were throwing in with the right people. I should mention that that conversation happened almost four years ago, and Zac and I still are in that small group today. **And those friends we did not intentionally choose? They are some of the closest friends that we have.**

Don't get me wrong: at many turns along the way, things between people in that group and us have been incredibly difficult. Especially at first, it was awkward. As in, AWKWARD.

I can have fun in a group of new people, no problem—but raise the stakes and dive into how life *really* is going, and man, do my walls go up fast. And now a bunch of perfect strangers were supposed to have access to my deepest thoughts? My habits? My desires? My spending patterns? My time? And give *comments* on these things? Yikes.

Had I not been so desperate to find my people, I probably would have bailed. Thankfully, I didn't bail. Thankfully, I stayed put. Thankfully, when the invitation came to engage in candid, authentic, long-term community, I whispered an earnest *yes*. **That one yes has changed everything.**

Of course, we have fun together. We do, but, but that's not the goal. I think we make each other better. I don't know if we would have naturally like been drawn to each other in a social setting, but I think because we've been so intentional and we've been committed to each other, there's a deeper friendship. We have chemistry, but that's not the primary thing that brought us together. What brought us together was a commitment to grow—we wanted to help each other grow and we wanted to grow ourselves. We all showed up, and we all brought our full selves, and we allowed ourselves to be sharpened. There were times I thought that Ellen, my now-good-friend from the group, didn't like me. It was a bumpy start. But I decided to take a risk: *I am going to be my full self.*

And once I did it, she did the same. We're close now. That was a scary day for me. But I had to choose: *I'm going to test this. I'm going to risk this. I'm not going to listen to the voice in my head that's telling me to resist.* And I felt like I got one of my dearest friends out of it. And so I'm so glad I didn't just walk away or pull back out of insecurity.

Let me assure you that today, I have my village. Since I moved here to Dallas, a handful of other friends have come into my life, too. It's diverse and intrusive, and they hold me up and together. **I love them, and they are in and out of my life most every minute of every day. And I want this for you, if you don't already have it. More importantly, God wants this for you.**

My suspicion? You want this, too.

TELL IT TO ME STRAIGHT

We are craving accountability. Accountability is one of those lost tastes of heaven that made God's plan for community work for the people in it. And this is not just listening to criticism from anyone and everyone or taking all unfounded theories to heart. It is building relationships and taking risks with people and allowing them to sharpen us.

People who live up close to each other have the prerogative to speak into each other's lives. To be a little bit of grit to sand off each other's edges. To push each other and call each other out in truth and grace and love.

I've noticed a trend in recent years regarding our need to be accepting and tolerant of people, literally no matter what. If we listen to what society tells us, then we will put tolerance at the tip-top of the list of things we must do to be a good friend these days.

To each her own.

Live your best life.

Honor your truth.

You do you.

Really though, the last thing you and I need is a friend group that does nothing more than co-sign our stupidity. If I'm about to career off a cliff and the only thing you choose to do is stand there cheering for me, we've got a problem. I don't need acceptance when I'm being a fool; I need help. And so do you.

It will take discernment and effort to return to these kinds of relationships that really build us—the kind that God had in mind for us to enjoy.

But we *can* return. We can swallow our pride and dare to be accountable to each other.

STUDY ::

Read Acts 2:40-47

▷ *What was the foundation of the early church? What launched it? (vv. 40–41)*

▷ *In verse 42 what were they devoted to together?*

▷ *How were they changed? (v. 43)*

▷ *And out of all of that, what did they do? How did they live? Make a list from verses 44-47a.*

▷ *What was the result of living like this? (v. 47b)*

> *Do you crave life together like this? How so? How do you wish you'd had someone telling it to you straight in the past?*

> *In what ways have we gotten away from this as followers of Christ today?*

CATCH ME, PLEASE

What if we are running from the thing we need most—namely, to be caught?

To be named and seen and noticed and corrected. It's not regular in our culture, but the Bible talks about it a *lot*:

". . . if anyone is caught in any transgression, you who are spiritual should restore him in a spirit of gentleness". (Galatians 6:1)

"Obey your leaders and submit to them, for they are keeping watch over your souls and will give an account . . .". (Hebrews 13:17)

"Let each one of you speak the truth with his neighbor, for we are members one of another". (Ephesians 4:25)

"If your brother sins against you, go and tell him his fault, between you and him alone. If he listens to you, you have gained your brother". (Matthew 18:15)

"Without counsel plans fail, but with many advisers they succeed". (Proverbs 15:22)

"Submit to one another out of reverence for Christ". (Ephesians 5:21 NIV)

These are only a few of the dozens and dozens of verses and passages that speak to this idea of submission, accountability, and both receiving and giving loving correction.

I'm often asked about what I think makes friendships work, about what I think "authentic community" actually is, and while there are several aspects to that vision, at the top of the list would be the practice of saying hard things and the practice of listening to and receiving those hard things.

"As iron sharpens iron, so one person sharpens another".
(Proverbs 27:17 NIV)

We have the opportunity to both sharpen and be sharpened, if only we'll see our relationships as the anvil that they are. And yet who in their right mind wants to sign up for being the piece of metal that's getting reshaped? Tortuous flames, the pounding against an unforgiving surface, the bending and prodding and pain. Nobody thinks they want that experience, but we do. We actually crave it. We just don't always know how to have it.

WHAT KEEPS US FROM ACCOUNTABILITY?

There is a bigger enemy to living this way than our discomfort: pride.

Pride is the great coverup for what we all know is really true. We are all sinners, in need of grace.

Adam and Eve eat the apple. Hide from God and then devise a plan. *Maybe He won't notice we are naked and ashamed if we put on these cute stylish little leaves!*

So they pull out their sewing machine, throw together little outfits, and come out of hiding with their heads held high.

"All good here!" they chime.

But God knows better.

Adam blames Eve.

Eve blames the snake.

Pride sinks them both.

Pride is our defense when we are accused. Our opinion, we are certain, is Bible truth. Our good works we set out to show we are a good person. Our achievements that mean we are justified. Our proof we wave around to show we aren't sinful. Pride says, *How dare she say that!* Or *How dare he criticize me!*

But nothing on earth is more freeing than just owning it. Being caught. Admitting we sin. Owning our mistakes. Laying down our defenses and proving ourselves, and joyfully resting in God's provision for our sins.

And let me tell you—people who live this way are my FAVORITES! They are self-deprecating and never defensive and fun and honest and free. And they can be you and me, if we accept that God's got us, and He's got the people around us.

GETTING SHARP

If you're committed to growing, you will start to see that anvil I mentioned not as punishment but as progress you desperately need. You will quit hiding and hedging. You will quit recoiling when questions are asked. You will quit pretending that you have it all together. You will let a little useful pounding into your life.

Scripture says we need this:

"See to it . . . that none of you has a wicked heart of unbelief that turns away from the living God. But exhort one another daily, as long as it is called today, so that none of you may be hardened by sin's deceitfulness". (Hebrews 3:12-13 BSB, emphasis added)

His way to keep us together and protect us from the enemy and sin is EACH OTHER.

Our people fighting for us and us fighting for them.

WHO ARE YOU, LORD? & WHAT DO YOU WANT FROM ME?

Read Scripture: 1 Peter 2:1–10. In light of what you read, answer the questions above.

PROJECT 1
UNCOVER

▷ *List the hesitations or fears you have in submitting to other people.*

WHAT'S GOING ON?	
WHY AM I WORRIED?	
WHAT PROBLEMS AM I FACING?	
HOW AM I INSECURE?	
WHAT SIN AM I FIGHTING?	
WHAT AM I LEARNING?	
WHAT AM I CONTROLLING?	

▷ *Spend some time journaling this week about what is really going on in your life. If you don't know what's going on, it's hard to ask for help.*

▷ *None of us likes to get our sin named and called out, so let's begin with INVITING this rather than seeking to do this for someone else.*

Many people overuse the verse, "as for those who persist in sin, rebuke them in the presence of all, so that the rest may stand in fear" (1 Timothy 5:20) and underuse the verse, "Why do you see the speck that is in your brother's eye, but do not notice the log that is in your own eye?" (Matthew 7:3). So be slow to call out other people's sin, and be quick to ask other people to call out your sin.

▷ *What would success look like for you in this category, based on your personality?*

▷ *What are you afraid of?*

▷ *What pressures do you feel to become something? Who is God actually calling you to become?*

PROJECT 2
YOUR ACCOUNTABILITY PLAN

Begin with answering this:

Who in your life has wisdom to speak into your life?

(Maybe it is a peer or somebody older. Remember that village life includes friends and mentors and a wider net of people who can speak wisdom into your life, not just your besties.)

1. Give permission to this person or people to tell the truth to you.

2. Ask them regularly: (a) What area do you see in my life that I need to grow? (b) What practices do I need in my life to mature? (c) Can you hold me accountable to this change?

3. Plan a follow-up. Plan a time you can revisit this conversation.

4. Ask them if you can hold them accountable for anything.

PROJECT 3
TELL THE TRUTH

I've shared in my other studies a saying I got from my home church in Dallas: "Say the last 2 percent." That's that card you're not playing—you're holding it close to your chest. You're okay sharing about certain struggles, but there's that last, little bit that's secret. Maybe we think *Oh, I'll take care of this myself. I'll work it out. I'll handle it—no one has to know.* But that part, the devil wants you to keep in the dark with him. If we don't play that card, we languish in our secrets. That last 2 percent is what gets us. But saying it out loud is what frees us for accountability. We can take those dark struggles captive and break their power. You are seen. Known. Loved.

So what is your last 2 percent? You choose to share or not to share, but you have to know what's there.

PROJECT 4
HAVE FUN

▷ *Write these five questions on pieces of paper, throw them in the middle of your friends, and give your most honest answer:*

▸ What's something you're not proud of?

▸ What's something you need help with?

▸ When was the last time you cried?

▸ What keeps you up at night?

▸ If you could change one thing about your life, what would it be?

CONCLUSION

THE DEEP WORK

In our way-too-invasive small group, we have gone *deep*. I mean, we show each other all of it. And yet I have never experienced a group of people fight for us like this group of people does.

Even with *money*. Early on, our group leader let us know we were going to share about finances. *Pardon?* They wanted specifics on purchases being considered, purchases that had been made, and overall financial standing. They wanted data—as in, spreadsheets were encouraged. I can't tell you how uncomfortable this made me. But stay with me here.

One of the couples was in the market for a new house, and so, as was the custom of this group, they brought all the information to the other couples. And then a massive conversation ensued.

People asked questions. People made observations. People offered alternatives for consideration. People prayed for clarity and wisdom on behalf of the prospective homebuyers. And as I sat there taking in all this activity, something almost tangible broke off within me. Something that felt a lot like fear.

Looking back over the past four years, Zac and I have run every major financial decision by our group. And while that may sound horrifying to you—"You tell them everything??"—it has been a tremendous source of peace in our lives, this knowledge that these fellow sojourners have our backs.

"But doesn't that information ever get used against you?" you ask.

I suppose it could someday.

Be wise. Choose safe people.

Weaponization is always possible, but so far, the benefits have outweighed the risks.

If this is done right, we love Jesus more, and our lives show that love to be real.

The truth is, when you add accountability to the necessary proximity and transparency we've addressed, you unleash a new level of potency in your life. You get sharper, more effective. You change. But if you skip this practice, you miss the whole point. Don't miss being sharpened by those you love.

SEE ::

Watch Video Session 5 now.
Use streaming code on inside cover or DVD.

SHARED MISSION

I have a friend who is a pastor in an underground church in the Middle East. He told me this story.

> "We have a saying in the Middle East that you don't know someone until you've gone on a trip with them and you've eaten with them. It's so true. The camaraderie. You don't see that in the West. When, for example, Corona hit the Middle East, the leaders and I all hunkered down in one house. The twenty of us with kids. You really bond when that happens. True discipleship doesn't happen out there—it happens in a home. True discipleship isn't something you do once a week. It's what you do every day, because that's when you get to know people—it's when you're with them during the good times and the bad times. When they're sick and when they're healthy. That's what builds true family. The blood of Christ makes us family, but we need to experience it together every day."

On mission together. Making disciples in our everyday moments. That's how it all began, too.

It started with Jesus and His village and His twelve people, and it spread out from there. They lived life together. And over the centuries, day by day, moment by moment, that's how the church has grown millions strong. Loving and living and working beside each other—toward a shared mission of millions saved and living in heaven with God forever. Intense. But real. And Mission is that next ingredient of God-intended community we are going to reclaim. It's fertile soil for friendship to grow.

There's a God-built longing inside each of us: to be about something other than our own individual success. We're going to be in heaven together forever and ever with the people we love, so why are we doing what we're doing? Our goal in connecting isn't just personal satisfaction, but to see people saved before Jesus returns.

If you want good friends, then run a race together, build a house together, cook a meal together, or live for the greatest mission together a human can have: giving God away together. Be on a mission.

GET BUSY!

Before the Fall, God gave us each other and then He gave us a mission—actual real-life, get-your-hands-dirty work to do. As Jesus ascended to heaven He said, "Go make more disciples." To the local church God's plan is spelled out, "For just as each of us has one body with many members," we read from the apostle Paul in Romans 12:4–5, "and these members do not all have the same function, so in Christ we, though many, form one body, and each member belongs to all the others."

He gives the people who follow Him a shared purpose and gifts that require dependence on each other to accomplish it.

We all crave this because we all were built for this.

Don't you want to be a part of something exciting and meaningful? Are you sick of living in your bubble of self-fulfillment and meeting your own small needs? What if you got to wake up every day with an assignment and a team of people by your side?

You can. This one truly is as simple as a change in perspective.

Anywhere could become a mission and anyone can become teammates.

I asked my Middle East pastor friend why he thinks the West has lost the art of living with mission and discipleship at the heart of the deepest friendships and daily life.

He said, "Because the West is all about individualism, convenience, and being comfortable. **Discipleship is inconvenient, uncomfortable, and very messy.**"

It's true. But it's beautiful. And we are going to fight to reclaim it. We're going to fight back against this individualistic culture that has intoxicated us into thinking that comfiness is happiness—because it's not. We have to get back to building the kingdom, messily, dirt under our fingernails . . . **together.** On a mission.

STUDY ::

Read Matthew 29:16-24

Jesus gave a final commission to His current and future disciples before He ascended to heaven: the Great Commission.

▷ *Write out verses 19 and 20a here:*

Underline any command words that God is asking us to do.

▷ *In your own words write out what Jesus has called us to do.*

Read Ephesians 4:14–16

▷ *What is God calling His church to leave?*

▷ *What is God calling His church to live?*

▷ *How is the church built up? (v. 16)*

▷ *What could happen if together we lived this way?*

▷ *What stops us from living this way?*

▷ *How would living this way change your everyday, work-a-day life?*

THE MASTER PLAN

Back in 1954, seminary professor Dr. Robert Coleman wrote a book called *The Master Plan of Evangelism*,[2] which outlines how Jesus went about his mission to save us. Apparently, Jesus' approach was pretty simple. It all revolved around doing mission—the Great Commission—together, as a part of everyday life. The Master's plan was ultimately an outline for our mission together. Let's dig into Dr. Coleman's main points and the Scriptures that inform them.

1. **Selection:** People were His method. The Master's plan started with Jesus focusing on a few men to disciple. He chose them on purpose because they had an attitude of willingness—and pretty much no other qualifications!

---

2. Robert E. Coleman, *The Master Plan of Evangelism* (Ada, MI: Revell, repackaged ed., 2020).

"Now when they saw the boldness of Peter and John, and perceived that they were uneducated, common men, they were astonished. And they recognized that they had been with Jesus". (Acts 4:13)

2. **Association:** He stayed with them. Essentially, He stuck around—even when they were getting it wrong. He stayed through the most cringeworthy things they did. He nurtured them along the path of the mission. It took time and togetherness. That's it.

"And you also will bear witness, because you have been with me from the beginning". (John 15:27)

Deep friends and community don't come off assembly lines either. They take time. And "getting with."

3. **Consecration:** He required obedience. The term obedience makes a lot of us stress out because we're not sure we're doing it right, and we see our shortcoming as loud and glaring and embarrassing. Thankfully, Jesus didn't see them that way. The disciples were following a Person, not a set of rules.

"So Jesus said to the Jews who had believed him, 'If you abide in my word, you are truly my disciples, and you will know the truth, and the truth will set you free'". (John 8:31–32)

We're abiding (staying) in Jesus and His teachings, and learning the truth along the way.

4. **Impartation:** He gave Himself away. Jesus taught by giving from God's inexhaustible supply. Coleman points out that He gave them peace, joy, His own glory, and His own life; and then He gave the Spirit, which we have today. Jesus prayed to keep giving it away, through you:

"O righteous Father, even though the world does not know you, I know you, and these know that you have sent me. I made known to them your name, and I will continue to make it known, that the love with which you have loved me may be in them, and I in them". (John 17:25–26)

5. **Demonstration:** He showed them how to live. Jesus demonstrated love, and says to us, "Now you try." He also showed us how to keep ourselves fueled through prayer and the word. Constantly, every day, as common as eating and breathing.

"Man shall not live by bread alone, but by every word that comes from the mouth of God". (Matthew 4:4)

6. **Delegation:** He assigned them work. Coleman points out that He "sent them forth" with the job of preaching and healing and living in community with others, starting with "kinsmen." They were to expect some hardship; that's why he put them in teams. Togetherness was the safety net.

"He called the twelve and began to send them out two by two". (Mark 6:7)

7. **Supervision:** He kept check on them. They met up regularly and worked it out as they went. They responded to situations and specific needs. They tried problem solving. And He always stepped in when they were stumped. When they got it right, He celebrated:

"I thank you, Father, Lord of heaven and earth, that you have hidden these things from the wise and understanding and revealed them to little children; yes, Father, for such was your gracious will". (Luke 10:21)

It wasn't by their own awesomeness, but by the Father's will that these "little children" were able to go out in His name and work in power on His mission.

8. **Reproduction:** He expected them to reproduce. Just as God told Adam and Eve to be fruitful and multiply, Jesus gave the same taste of heaven to His community of followers. The kingdom of God, He said, is like

"the smallest of all seeds, but when it has grown it is larger than all the garden plants and becomes a tree, so that the birds of the air come and make nests in its branches". (Matthew 13:32)

We are the plan, folks. It's us. Coleman says:

"This was the way His church was to win—through the dedicated lives of those who knew the Savior so well that His Spirit and method constrained them to tell others. As simple as it may seem, this was the way the gospel would conquer. He had no other plan."

That's the Master's Plan, and our mission. It's based around togetherness. As we learn how to be "with" and "together" with our people, there is no better plan to follow.

Some of you might be thinking, *What does it look like to be on a mission? I don't know what I'm good at. I don't know what God wants me to do.* **There is a need right in front of you. You don't have to go find some**

mysterious calling or mission field. It's right where you are. What is the need in your neighborhood? What is the need in your kids' friend's lives? What is the need in your kids? What is the need in your marriage? What is the need in your friends' lives? Look in front of you and meet the need. Most of us don't wake up in the morning wanting to serve other people or head right out into evangelism (unless you're an enneagram 2), but it's really delightful to help people on any kind of mission. It's the best way to live. **When we serve others, we see that there's a greater plan for our lives than building a comfortable life. And we're better together.**

WHO ARE YOU, LORD? & WHAT DO YOU WANT FROM ME?

Read Ecclesiastes 4:9–12. In light of what you read, write your answers to the questions above.

PROJECT 1
DRAW

▷ *Draw what it would look like living on mission with your friends.*

Look back at Ephesians 4:16 if you need some inspiration.

PROJECT 2
TIME INVENTORY

▷ *There are 168 hours in a week. Let's take inventory of how you are spending your time.*

ACTIVITY	HOURS SPENT

What do you need to:

1. Add (do you have a significant amount of margin?)

2. Subtract (are you too busy for people?)

3. Invite + Include (how can you intentionally build your close friends into your week?)

Hopefully you're building traction with a few of these friends who you want to continue with. Or maybe you still don't see a lot of potential, and you might invite new friends to into your life. Either way, put yourself out there with a few people and trust the process. You're doing stuff, so why not add more good stuff to the stuff you're already doing?

PROJECT 3
REFLECT

▶ *Reflect on a time you lived on mission. Was it as part of a team? A group project? What were your relationships like with those people?*

▶ *What good elements would you like to nurture as you step out on mission with your people now?*

PROJECT 4
FIND A CAUSE

Friendship and community centered around other people and a bigger mission is the most satisfying and bonding type of relationship. And guess what? If you are a follower of Jesus . . .

▷ *You have a built-in mission that is embedded in every type of job, neighborhood, hobby, club, and school: share the love of God.*

▷ *You have a village, a team, to be on that mission with you: your local church.*

> ▷ What is your church up to?

> ▷ How can you find out?

WHAT I'M UP TO . . .	WHAT MY CHURCH IS UP TO . . .
(causes that move me, the way and places I spend time)	(programs, outreach, service, mission statements, etc.)

Where there's crossover, how could you get involved? If there's none, could you dream with a sister in Christ and start something?

CONCLUSION

THE LOCAL MISSION

You may know that I lead a non-profit called IF:Gathering. We build tools and experiences to help women connect with God. Our team feels more like a family than coworkers, evidenced at this moment by the endless text stream we're all on. We do life together in deep ways. We call out each other's sin. We share meals, even when the gatherings have nothing to do with work. My kids count many of the long-time teammates of IF:Gathering as aunties and friends. **We do life together.** And we're on a shared mission, which has cemented us together.

Years ago, we decided that the big Gatherings of thousands of women were good, but the real stuff would happen with the small groups. So we started If:Local—a resource to help gather you together on mission.

We thought, the way the world changes is life-on-life. We wanted to help you and to serve you and to put tools in your hands, in your places, because we believe in you. We think you are the best person to reach your neighbors, to reach your friends, to reach your fellow students on your campus. They don't need to come hear a fancy speaker. Small groups are equally viable. You can check out If:Local and join a mission that way—you're invited. Or, just as wonderfully, you can just look up and look around and see the possibilities where you are. No matter what, know that God is already working. He's inviting you to join. The friendships you gain along the way? They're a blessing on the way to the greatest thing possible—the saving of the world. Believe it.

SEE ::

Watch Video Session 6 now.
Use streaming code on inside cover or DVD.

CONSISTENCY

Community. Togetherness. People in your business. Living life like this, you are for sure going to come to a moment in the very near future when you are going to want to bolt. Mark my words.

During quarantine, my sister-in-law Ashley called and asked to talk. It sounded serious, but I assumed it was something difficult happening in her life, not something between her and me. I just didn't see it coming.

She picked me up, and we drove to a park and sat in the car. She cried as she told me a few things I had said recently that had hurt her. She talked about how hard it was to bring this to me but how the candor was necessary. She didn't want to slowly start pulling back from me. She didn't want to "quit me," she said.

The two words brought waves of fear. Panic. *Was I about to lose another friend? And one who was a family member, no less?*

Shame came in and stayed. *What on earth had I done?*

I keep hurting people!

I hurt people without even realizing it and most often it is the people very closest to me, who I love very most.

I breathed in and out. I listened. I waited for my turn to speak.

We both were faced with a choice as we sat in the car on that beautiful day.

Self-protect.

Blame.

Pull back.

Even walk away.

Or . . .

Fight.

Fight it out, fight for each other, fight to understand and fight to *stay*.

After all the hurt was laid out, she said, "I am staying. This is me, fighting for us."

In the days that followed, I confess that I didn't feel safe with Ashley anymore. Why was that my internal reaction? In her bringing this hurt and conflict to me, she was proving three things:

> ▷ She was safe.

> ▷ She loved me.

> ▷ She was committed to me.

She was not angry; she was hurt, and she wanted restoration.

A few days later, Ashley and I went to dinner. I looked at her and said, "I love you so much. Telling me what you told me was such a gift to me. I am sorry. I was wrong. I am so sorry I hurt you. I never want to hurt you, but I did, and I will again. But still, I want you to feel safe with me. Tell me how to do that better, please."

The next thing she said was pure magic. Ashley gave me two super-easy, simple ways that I could love her well. And in that moment, I realized I didn't need to quit, and I didn't need to spiral in fear, and I didn't need to self-protect.

What I needed was to grow.

When we stay, we grow. We learn the art of reconciliation. We fight it out and work it out and cry it out and show up again the next day.

See, God made consistency a part of His model for community, because we can't grow something good if we keep pulling up the roots of what we've planted over and over. We have to leave them to grow into something big and magnificent. But in the meantime, we just keep showing up. And as we reconcile with each other, we reflect God's ultimate goal in sending Jesus to us: to reconcile us to Himself.

STUDY ::

Read Revelation 21 and 22

We began in Genesis and we are ending in Revelation.

Eden was ruined, but God is building a new city with a redeemed people to dwell again with Him forever. Let's read about it.

Read the passage once more and this time jot down descriptions about this new holy city:

▷ *What will it contain?*

▷ *What will be true of us?*

▷ *What does God say about Himself?*

▷ *Who will be there and who will not be there?*

▷ *How do these words make you want to live today?*

ONE ANOTHERS

While writing this study, I dreamed of you in your places, actually taking these practices from village life and applying them in your apartment complexes, in your neighborhoods, in your dorms or condos.

I pictured you by fires, and opening doors to new friends, asking better questions and picking up a mission with a few people you love. I even pictured you fighting! Yep. **Because I've never had a truly intimate friendship that was free from conflict.**

I pictured you fighting and pictured you coming back to the table, back to each other.

I am asking you and I believe that God is asking us to let people into our daily lives, into our deepest struggles, into our sin, into our routines, into our work, and into our dreams.

Throughout this study we've looked at verses I like to call "one anothers"— the wisdom God gives us on how to be together. Let's collect them all here. God is telling us to:

"Exhort one another every day, as long as it is called 'today,' that none of you may be hardened by the deceitfulness of sin". (Hebrews 3:13)

"Bear one another's burdens, and so fulfill the law of Christ". (Galatians 6:2)

"Comfort one another, agree with one another, live in peace; and the God of love and peace will be with you". (2 Corinthians 13:11)

"Stir up one another to love and good works". (Hebrews 10:24)

"Be kind to one another, tenderhearted, forgiving one another, as God in Christ forgave you". (Ephesians 4:32)

If God is commanding you to forgive each other, then that means you and I are living in close enough proximity that I can actually reach you . . . and also hurt you. When He says that we are to bear one another's burdens, this means I am close enough to you to get up under that burden and actually relieve some of the load. How can I confess my sin to or admonish you unless I can look you in the eye and tell you? **You and I have to be close if these commandments are going to be kept.**

We must become people who come close.

We must become people who engage.

We must become people who choose to stay.

My friend, pastor Halim Suh, and I were talking about all this, and he made the good point that these "one anothers" can't be kept as an individual. The community is necessary to keep God's commands. The Bible says that God's commands are there for our good and human flourishing (Psalm 119), so it's clear here that we can only flourish together. God has built us to where we can't flourish without one another.

That's where the church comes in. Listen—I am so painfully aware of all the ways the church has hurt its people. You have told me things that break my heart, things that never, ever should have happened. And it is the source of rivers of tears. So it is with great tenderness that I ask you all to remember Jesus came to redeem the church, to heal it as He heals those of us within it. Let's pursue that together. The fact is, the only way I as an individual can receive the fullness of God and experience all of His benefits is within the context of the community of the church. Sometimes I tend to think obeying God and living a holy life means that I have to work on myself and my character. But Jesus was more interested in the character of the church. If we truly love God, of course it should be the desire of our heart to experience and know Him. And the way we know Him is not just individual, one-on-one relationships. I experience more of God within the context of the church.

STAY AT THE TABLE

Throughout history, breaking bread together around the table has always represented reconciliation and healing.

Jesus is betrayed by Judas. The events leading to His crucifixion are set in motion. Jesus will be betrayed and hurt by nearly every one of his closest people sitting around the table and later He will die. But in the midst of the hurt and rejection He must have been experiencing, He pulls out bread and breaks it. He pours wine; He and His friends drink it.

"Now as they were eating, Jesus took bread, and after blessing it broke it and gave it to the disciples, and said, 'Take, eat; this is my body.' And he took a cup, and when he had given thanks he gave it to them, saying, 'Drink of it, all of you, for this is my blood of the covenant, which is poured out for many for the forgiveness of sins'". (Matthew 26:26)

The ultimate table of reconciliation had been set. Built on the broken body and spilled blood of our Savior. It's why we can forgive. It's why we can come to the table together with other sinners. We can, because He did. We can, because He made a way for us to be right with Him and right with each other.

I have community. **My biggest issue with community is usually that I hurt someone or that they hurt me.** It is a regular storyline. I mean, weekly the conflict has to be resolved in my life, and it's because that's just part of healthy community. **The hurt is part of the health**—it's weird to think about, but it's true.

I'm part of a huge church that has small groups within it. We're trying to make it so the parts of the body of Christ all know each other and work together. It's hard. It's messy. But we have to keep coming back to the table, because we know that Jesus had a vision for this. He's redeeming us individually and as a church.

We're looking toward eternity described in Revelation, and we want to model heaven here. Pastor Halim pointed out that there is value to gathering as a big church—a massive group of people. That's the picture of Revelation: a crowd and multitude upon multitude shouting and praising God. It's a rehearsal of the heavenlies. The kind of worship that we're going to give to God, and He's going to call us into from every tongue, tribe, and nation in a number that no one can number (Revelation 7). That's the whole point.

Then when you sit down with your missional community or your inner circle, or your village, and you're crying and sharing things, and you really do know each other, that's the other side of the coin. Big table, little table. We know one another. We carry one another's burdens. We need both. They're tastes of heaven. We are called to set tables of all sizes and return to them again and again. We're called to stay and enjoy the feast.

WHO ARE YOU, LORD? & WHAT DO YOU WANT FROM ME?

Read Ephesians 3:16-19. In light of what you read, answer the questions above.

PROJECT 1
FORGIVENESS

▷ *Who are the people you're going to commit to? Have a DTR.*

▷ *Define for yourself a guideline for the forgiveness you'll inevitably need:*

Why I'm tempted to quit people:

▸ I want to run when . . .

My commitments to stay:

▸ I choose to stay because . . .

Explore what could hold you back from commitment, so you know exactly what's going on and how to move forward.

WHAT AM I AFRAID OF WHEN IT COMES TO COMMITMENT?	WHY AM I AFRAID?

WHY I DON'T NEED TO BE AFRAID: (FEEL FREE TO LIST SCRIPTURE FROM THIS STUDY)	WHAT CAN I DO TO ACT FEARLESSLY?

PROJECT 2
COMMIT TO YOUR FEW

It's time to build your weekly rhythm with your people.

Commit to a day and a time with a group of friends every week for the next six months.

1. Pick your people.

2. Invite them to gather more regularly.

3. Pick your time and location and keep it consistent.

4. Decide how long you're going to commit to each other—it doesn't need to be indefinite.

5. Decide what questions you're going to answer in your weekly time together. Here are some we use:

   What is happy?

   What is hard?

   How are you growing?

   Who are you investing in?

PROJECT 3
FIGHT RIGHT

Conflict is inevitable—if we're doing things right. We can handle conflict in a way that honors and glorifies God to the rest of the world.

1. **We keep short accounts.**

   Say no to grudges. We can do this because our hope is heaven, where our citizenship truly is. **We are satisfied in our relationship with God so we can be content with people being people.** We can let them disappoint us and just let it go. Some hurts are just misunderstandings.

   ▷ *When have you made assumptions in the past and blown up a whole narrative out of some little thing someone did or said? How does it feel when you find out you're not working in reality?*

   ▷ *How would just letting go quicker avoid these situations?*

   ▷ *How have you or someone you loved kept short accounts/let things go for the good of themselves and everyone?*

   ▷ *With whom/in what situations can you resolve to do this more?*

2. We assume the best.

Give it time. Walk away from it and sleep on it and if you notice you can't let that thing go, then go to that person. Ask them what they meant by what they said. You might have misunderstood them, so give them space to explain. Assume the best of people.

▷ When has someone done this for you?

▷ When do you wish you had done this for someone else?

▷ How can you be ready to do this for someone you're thinking of right now?

3. We are quick to apologize.

I can't tell you how many times people have brought me something that hurt them, and I didn't even know I'd sinned in their eyes. There was no ill intention, no purposeful hurt, and I didn't even realize I said or did the things I so clearly said or did. That doesn't matter. They felt hurt, specifically by me. **I take responsibility for hurting them, even if I didn't mean to.**

▷ Apologize.

▷ Ask what you can do to make amends.

▷ Don't say much else. (It's too tempting to go down the explanation/excuse road and hurt them further.)

▷ Let God be your defender. Act out of His abundance.

▷ *What's the worst apology you've experienced/heard? Why did it fail?*

▷ *What's the best apology you've received? How did it help?*

▷ *Envision a person you may need to apologize to. (Hint: it will inevitably be someone you're closest too.) Visualize going through this four-step apology. How can you prepare to be a good apologizer?*

PROJECT 4
DREAM

▷ *Write a letter to yourself below. Tell yourself your hopes for your relationships for the coming year. How do you want to shift and to grow? What is it going to take to get there?*

CONCLUSION

FEAST WITH US

When my sister-in-law Ashley committed to staying with me, not quitting me, and bringing her hurt to me, it was the greatest act of love. We are solid now. We may have to do this again and again, but we'll keep showing up, keep sitting down at the table with one another. And we'll be sitting together at a table in eternity, too.

Revelation describes a "wedding feast of the Lamb" (Revelation 19:9). There's going to be a table in heaven, and instead of brokenness we'll bring to it joy. What we're building here will last into that place, so let's start sitting down and staying now. It starts small and simple and so awkward, but just like all the tastes of heaven on earth, it is worth reclaiming.

We stay, because we expect growth and we expect the help of the Holy Spirit.

The moment you decide to stay and accept your people for who they are instead of trying to get them to change or wishing they were different . . .

> ▷ the moment you look for ways to serve instead of constantly expecting things from them . . .

> ▷ the moment you watch for opportunities to speak an encouraging word instead of questioning their every decision . . .

> ▷ the moment you seek out chances to love them well instead of fearing awfulness or awkwardness in your exchanges with them . . .

Might be the moment when you will see your family, your people, and your church changed.

I'll say it yet again: Your people might be right in front of you. But even if they aren't today, let me tell you the greatest news: the one friend I have found to be most consistent, the one who sees me at my worst and still loves me, is Jesus.

And if you know Him, He calls you His friend, "I no longer call you servants, because a servant does not know his master's business. Instead, I have called you friends." That longing we have to be fully known, fully accepted, on mission, seen, loved, not alone—it is wholly answered in Him. Jesus is my best friend.

Maybe you aren't with Him yet. That's okay. When Kate was five years old, she was telling us about her best friend when her punk older brother shamed her by saying, "Jesus is supposed to be your best friend."

She responded, "Well, I am just getting to know Him."

If that's you, that's okay. But I can tell you this, Jesus makes the best friend. He has never ignored me, cut me out, shamed me, or rolled His eyes at me. Not once. He always listens, always cares, always tells me truth. He is always there. He is safe and encouraging and always challenges me and makes me better too.

You are never alone. You have Jesus. And He has you.

But He wants more for you. More for us. A team of people to run with each day, to love Him together and love each other through the hard. He wants this for you. I want this for you.

It's worth the fight. Run on. Love on.

Find your people, and never let them go.

SEE ::

Watch Video Session 7 now.
Use streaming code on inside cover or DVD.

LEADER'S GUIDE

PHOTO BY: MESHALI MITCHELL

Dear leader,

I am excited to partner with you in your efforts to pour into the lives of women! I pray that these few short pages will help to equip and prepare you to lead this study. Many of you may have led plenty of groups in the past, or perhaps this is the first you've led. Whichever the case, this is a spiritual calling and you are entering spiritual places with these women—and spiritual callings and places need spiritual power.

My husband, Zac, always says, "Changed lives change lives." If you are not first aware of your own need for life change, the women around you won't see their need. If you allow God into the inner struggles of your heart, the women following you will be much more likely to let Him into theirs. Thank you for shining the way.

This is not a study for people wanting to keep the status quo and just maybe pick up a few new friends along the way. This study messes with you because it invites us to change our whole concept of independence, loneliness, and vulnerability and live with freedom from the isolation and loneliness that our enemy wants for us. I want a life where, instead of constant loneliness with brief moments of connection and community, I have constant connection with only brief moments of loneliness. I want to flip the script on our culture. Don't you?

Together, we can do this. We can and we will encourage one another, hold each other accountable, and start to tear down the walls of pain and injury that keep us apart, focusing individually and collectively on Jesus. That is where we will find true freedom. Loneliness and isolation isn't "just the human condition." We do have power to change it! Let's take a bold step together toward the community we were meant for.

Grateful,

Jennie

PREPARING YOURSELF TO LEAD

1. Pray

Pray for yourself: Pray that you will be led by the Spirit. Pray that you would lead with wisdom, compassion, discernment, and urgency. Pray fervently and continuously.

Pray for your women, that they would:

▷ embrace God's plan for community and be inspired to open up and connect

▷ have hearts that are teachable and moldable

▷ be transformed by God's Word and His Spirit.

2. Lean on God

Don't lead this Bible study in your own power. Allow the Holy Spirit to lead every moment—your preparation, your facilitation, your follow-up.

Don't just teach what's on the page. Allow the Spirit freedom to work outside the boundaries of your plan and agenda.

Depend on God for the results. Don't try to manufacture moments or experiences. Keep in mind your responsibility is to be obedient and faithful to teach the Word. The results are left to God.

Teach out of the overflow of your own walk with God. You can't pour out much truth from an empty pitcher. Spend time daily with the Savior in an intimate love relationship with Him. Let Him pour into you before you pour out on others.

3. Be Vulnerable

There will be times you will need to open up and share your life. This will help others feel safe to share. But don't feel like you have to share every detail. You don't. Share what is necessary, guided by the Holy Spirit.

4. Listen, But Also Lead

Allow women to share their struggles and do your best not to interrupt. However, you will need to guide the conversation. You will need to include all women in the discussion. You will need to continue to steer the conversation back to the truth of God's Word.

5. Model Trust

Don't be a "do as I say" leader. Be the example. Apply what you have learned and are learning through the study.

THE STUDY: SESSION TOOLS AND FORMAT

Find Your People is designed to work in various types of venues and locations, including homes, dorm rooms, workplaces, or churches. Whether you find yourself leading a large group of women at church or a few neighbors in your home, the study is designed for small groups of women to share and process truth. I suggest a maximum number of eight in your group. If you are leading a large group at church, divide into smaller groups and enlist women to lead each small group.

WHAT'S IN THE BOX:

STUDY. One copy of the Bible study guide. A streaming video access code is included with each study guide on the inside front cover.

SEE. Seven sessions of video teaching on DVD or streaming using the access code printed on the inside cover of the study guide.

ASK. One set of Conversation Cards.

SESSION TOOLS AND HOW TO USE THEM

STUDY. Every participant will need a Bible study guide. Distribute the books at your first group meeting and walk participants through them. Plot out the weekly Study section, followed by the Projects. These can be completed in one sitting or spaced throughout the week. The lessons in the book (except for the Introduction lesson) should be completed between group meetings.

The lessons are interactive, designed to help women study Scripture for themselves and apply it to their lives. The Projects in the Bible study guide will provide creative options for applying Scripture. Some of these Experiences may push the women outside their comfort zones. Encourage them to be brave and tackle the challenge. Make sure to discuss the Projects at each group meeting.

SEE. Watch the short, engaging video teaching to introduce the lesson, set the tone for your time together, and challenge women to apply Scripture. If your group members want to take notes, encourage them to use the Notes page opposite each SEE title page. Each study guide includes a personal access code to Streaming Video on the inside front cover. This is perfect for women who miss a group gathering, want to re-watch any of the video teaching, or if your group needs to meet on shortened time.

ASK. The Conversation Cards provide a unique way to jumpstart honest discussion. Each week's cards are labeled with the appropriate lesson title and can be used after the video or teaching time. The following is a suggested step-by-step way to use the cards.

▷ Lay out the cards for the specific week with the questions facing up.

▷ Direct each woman to take a card.

▷ Go over the Ground Rules each week. (Ground rules are found on page xx and on the back of the Instruction card.)

▷ Begin by laying out the Scripture Card for that specific lesson.

▷ Allow each woman to ask the question on the card she selected. Provide adequate time for women to respond to the question.

Don't feel pressured to read and answer each question. Be sensitive to the leading of the Holy Spirit and your time constraints.

NOTE.

Make use of this leader's guide to facilitate a great Bible study experience for your group. It will help you point women to the overarching theme for each lesson and will give you specific suggestions on how to share the truth and foster discussion.

SESSION FORMAT

This seven-session study is designed to go deep very quickly, so it's flexible when considering the length of your group sessions. It can be led in a church spread out over a couple of hours, or in a break room over a one-hour lunch. However, the more time you can allow for discussion, the better. When the group is given deep questions and space to reflect and respond, you'll be surprised by the depth and beauty of the conversations.

You will be the best judge of what time and format works for your group. However, here is a suggested schedule for each group meeting.

1. OPEN—Personal study discussion *(15–35 minutes)*

After a warm welcome and opening prayer, provide time for the women to share and discuss their personal reflections from the study of Scripture and the Projects. If you have more than eight in your group, break into smaller groups for this discussion.

2. SEE—Video Teaching *(18–20 minutes)*

Use the video to lay the foundation for the week's lesson and transition to the Conversation Cards. Feel free to provide supplemental teaching for your group.

3. ASK—Conversation Cards *(25–75 minutes)*

Allow time for women to ask and discuss the question on each card. If you need an extra set of cards, they are available for purchase from your favorite online retailer.

4. CLOSE—Closing *(5–10 minutes)*

Pray as a group and encourage everyone to engage the Study before meeting again.

TIPS FOR LEADING YOUR GROUP

Always encourage the group members to abide by the following Ground Rules for discussion. These rules can be found below, on the back of the Instruction Card, and on page 5 of this Bible study book.

BE CONCISE

Share your answer to the questions while protecting others' time for sharing. Be considerate. Don't be afraid to share with the group, but try not to dominate the conversation.

KEEP GROUP MEMBERS' STORIES CONFIDENTIAL

Your group members will want to share sensitive and personal information with you, not with your husband or other friends. Protect each other by not allowing anything shared in the group to leave the group.

RELY ON SCRIPTURE FOR TRUTH

Conventional, worldly wisdom has value, but it is not absolute truth. Only Scripture provides that. In your times of discussion, be careful not to equate good advice with God's Truth.

NO COUNSELING

Work together to protect the group by not directing all attention toward solving one person's problem. This is the place for confessing and discovery and paply truth together as a group. However, at times a member may need to dig even deeper with an outside counselor or talk with a friend outside of small group time. If that is you, don't be afraid to ask for help, or be sure and follow up with a member of the group.

WHEN TO REFER

Some of the women in your group may be dealing with issues beyond your ability to help. If you sense that a woman may need more extensive help, refer her to speak with your pastor or a trained Christian counselor. Maintain the relationship and follow up with her to make sure she is getting the care needed. you or someone else in your group may need to walk with her through this season of her life. As we have said many times, be sensitive to the Holy Spirit's leading as you love and offer hope to the women in your group.

TYPES OF LEARNERS

Hopefully, you will be blessed to be leading this study with a group diverse in age, experience, and style. While the benefits of coming together as a diverse group to discuss God outweigh the challenges by a mile, there are often distinctions in learning styles. Just be aware and consider some of the differences in two types of learning styles that may be represented. (These are obviously generalizations, and each woman as an individual will express her own unique communication style, but in general these are common characteristics.)

SESSION 1

INTRODUCTION: GOD'S VISION FOR COMMUNITY

Note to Leader: The teaching format for this session is different than the other sessions because it is the first group time and there is no personal study to review.

1. OPEN

Welcome the women to your group and take a few moments for introductions. Briefly share about yourself and allow the other women to do the same. After introductions, lead the group in prayer.

Distribute the Bible study guides to group members and go over the Instructions and Expectations on page 4. Explain and show the women their individual access to Streaming Video so everyone can keep up with the study, regardless of an unavoidable missed gathering.

2. SEE

View the Session 1 video: "INTRODUCTION: GOD'S VISION FOR COMMUNITY."

3. ASK.

Transition to the Conversation Cards for discussion. The cards for this week are labeled "Introduction" on the front. Lead women to choose, answer, and discuss the questions on the cards. (You can review the instructions for using the cards in "SESSION FORMAT" on page 172.)

4. CLOSE

Close by asking the women to write down three things:

> one thing they learned from this session;

> one reason they are excited about this study;

> one question they have moving forward.

Briefly discuss their responses. Do so with little or no commentary, but paying close attention to the answers. If time allows, close by praying specifically for each woman in your group, using one of each woman's responses as the focus of your prayer for her.

Encourage women to complete Session 2 Study and Projects before the next group meeting.

"Your kingdom come, your will be done, on earth as it is in heaven". (Matthew 6:10)

SESSION 2

THE DISRUPTION OF COMMUNITY?

MAIN IDEA: It's terrifying to need people, but we were made for that. But something got broken along the way, and it's influencing every part of our relationships and friendships today.

In this session we will look at how we get past our shame about being "needy"—how we can start to get real about our mess and be vulnerable with each other. We will discover why we tend to cover ourselves with relational fig leaves, and how that has played out in the Bible. We will also craft a vision of God's original, perfect plan for community—and how we can get it back from the enemy who is dead set on destroying it.

Here are some general goals and thoughts for your time together this week:

1. Identify and define some of the the ways our culture has embraced isolation.

2. Discover how the Gospel is engineered to deal with shame.

3. Discuss the things God says about who He is, and how He invites us into relationship with Him.

Because of God's grace, His gospel, his power, we can come out of hiding and take a risk on loving others. While things are broken now, we get to participate in God's restoration of the world.

MAIN GOAL: Lead people to an honest evaluation of the source of separation in their relationship with God and with others, and encourage them to rediscover the freeing truth of the Gospel.

1. OPEN

Begin by reviewing the personal study from last week. Here are some suggested places to focus as you review:

▷ What truths stood out to you from the story of God's original plan for community in Genesis?

▷ How does John 8:36 speak to your own experience with shame?

▷ Share their responses to Project 4.

▷ What else stood out to you from the lesson and scripture that you want to learn, treasure, and/or apply?

2. SEE

Watch the video session "The Disruption of Community."

3. ASK

Transition to the Conversation Cards to continue your discussion. The cards for this week are labeled "Session 2" on the front. Lead women to choose, answer, and discuss the questions on the cards. (You can review the instructions for using the cards in "SESSION FORMAT" on page 172.)

4. CLOSE

Ask: "What is one change you need to make in your life because of what you experienced this week?" Encourage women to choose a partner and share their answers to that question with each other. Then challenge them to pray for each other to have the strength and courage to make that change.

Encourage women to complete Session 3 Study and Projects before the next group meeting.

"Then the Lord God said, 'It is not good that the man should be alone; I will make him a helper fit for him'". (Genesis 2:18)

SESSION 3

PROXIMITY

MAIN IDEA: So many of us find ourselves surrounded by strangers as we go about our business, heads down and distracted. But what if God orchestrated our daily run-ins to blossom into friendships?

Here are some general goals and thoughts for your time together this week:

1. Create awareness of the way we interact with people in our everyday, casual encounters.

2. Create a dissatisfaction with the things the world throws at us to keep us distracted, from the people around us, like busyness, phones, distraction, etc.

3. What does it look like to live in proximity? To be strengthened by those right around us? To welcome emotional closeness with those we're physically close with?

God wants to bring us back to a together way of life. We can dwell with each other, because He dwells with us.

MAIN GOAL: Energize people to find a new way of "with"ness—to open their eyes to those in proximity to them. As we observe the physical boundaries of our lives and dwelling places, may we become curious and excited about getting to know what is at our fingertips already. Spark bravery to initiate with others.

1. OPEN

   Begin by reviewing the personal study from last week. Here are some suggested places to focus as you review:

▷ Discuss he readings about God's dwelling places and Jesus' life in proximity. What does that say about God?

▷ Which people came to mind as you read about God's plan for proximity?

▷ What was God speaking to you through Acts 17:26–27?

▷ Have women share their village maps from Project 1.

▷ What else stood out to you from the lesson and Scripture that you need to learn, treasure, and/or apply?

2. SEE

Watch video session "Proximity."

3. ASK

Transition to the Conversation Cards to continue your discussion. The cards for this week are labeled "Session 3" on the front. Lead women to choose, answer, and discuss the questions on the cards. (You can review the instructions for using the cards in "SESSION FORMAT" on page 172.)

4. CLOSE

Circle your group and hold hands Encourage them to be closely connected ot Jesus and to each other this week. Close with prayer.

Encourage women to complete Session 4 Study and Projects before the next group meeting.

"God made from one man every nation of mankind to live on all the face of the earth, having determined allotted periods and the boundaries of their dwelling place, that they should seek God, and perhaps feel their way toward him and find him". (Acts 17:26-27)

SESSION 4

TRANSPARENCY

MAIN IDEA: We build walls to keep us safe, but they can keep out the good things in life as well. God urges us out from behind our walls, toward transparency, vulnerability, and all the good things that come with taking the risk for connection.

Here are some general goals and thoughts for your time together this session:

▷ Help women to see that there are better options than living behind walls.

▷ If we know God and trust Him we will be empowered to take His help and have the bravery to come out from behind our rickety walls

▷ Every time we notice ourselves building a wall, we can look to God's solution instead.

▷ It's okay to be awkward. We're going to have to go first sometimes.

▷ We weren't meant to be alone in the dark. God wants so much more for us, and for those He's put in our paths.

MAIN GOAL: Lead people to a dissatisfaction with the walls we build, and start to see the beautiful possibilities of living with transparency.

1. OPEN

   Begin by reviewing the personal study from last week.

   Here are some suggested places to focus as you review:

   ▷ What were the differences between walled-in cultures and those that don't have that luxury?

   ▷ What did you feel as you read (or reread) Romans 8?

   ▷ Which project stood out to you most this session?

   ▷ What else stood out to you from the lesson and Scripture that you need to learn, treasure, and/or apply?

2. SEE

   Watch the video session "Transparency."

3. ASK

   Transition to the Conversation cards to continue your discussion. The cards for this week are labeled "Session 4" on the front. Lead women to choose, answer, and discuss the questions on the cards. (You can review the instructions for using the cards in "SESSION FORMAT" on page 172.)

4. CLOSE

Close by sharing a personal story about your own walls, and how you've been led to tear them down. Ask if any group member is going through a tough time with tran right now. If one or more women indicate this is true in their lives, circle around them and pray for them.

Encourage women to complete Session 5 Study and Projects before the next group meeting.

> "There is therefore now no condemnation for those who are in Christ Jesus". (Romans 8:1)

SESSION 5

ACCOUNTABILITY: THE CHURCH

MAIN IDEA: We crave accountability—people up in our business and making us sharper—because it's how we grow as people. As we let go of our pride, we can accept the kind of help we need.

Here are some general goals and thoughts for your time together this session:

> ▷ Explain the concept of accountability as it was practiced in the early church.

> ▷ Awaken the need for friendships that do more than affirm us

> ▷ Underscore the value of saying and hearing hard things with grace.

> ▷ Discover how pride keeps us from sharpening

▷ God's plan to keep us safe from the enemy is worked out through each other. Let's fight for each other.

MAIN GOAL: Lead people to recognize the ways they've let pride isolate them, and lead them to the kind of relationships that sharpen us, remaining open to accountability.

1. OPEN

Begin by reviewing the personal study from last week. Here are some suggested places to focus as you review:

▷ Talk about the list of verses emphasizing counsel, getting caught, and accountability. What do they spark?

▷ Discuss the cultural barriers we tend to feel toward things like submission, correction, and accountability to others.

▷ Share your charts from Project 1. What's your biggest worry?

▷ Discuss your accountability plans Where do your women most desire to be held accountable?

▷ What lease stood out to you from the lesson and Scripture that you need to learn, treasure, and/or apply?

2. SEE

Watch the video for Session 5, "Accountability."

3. ASK

Transition to the Conversation cards to continue your discussion. The cards for this week are labeled "Session 5" on the front. Lead women to choose, answer, and discuss the questions on the cards. (You can review the instructions for using the cards in "SESSION FORMAT" on page 172.)

4. CLOSE

Challenge each member of your group to pray a prayer for sharpening, such as, "Lord, send me people to sharpen me and for me to sharpen in return, like iron on iron." Encourage them to write the prayer in their book or Bible and date it. Emphasize that this is not a prayer to pray lightly. Provide a quiet moment for them to consider this challenge, then close with prayer.

Encourage women to complete Session 6 Study and Projects before the next group meeting.

"As iron sharpens iron, so one person sharpens another". (Proverbs 27:17)

SESSION 6

SHARED MISSION: DISCIPLESHIP

MAIN IDEA: We are already on a mission. As we invite people into our missions, and join others', we find teammates and deep connection.

Here are some general goals and thoughts for your time together this session:

> Reignite that innate desire we all have to be a part of something bigger than just our little stuff.

▷ Focus on the long view: There's nothing wrong with wanting to make a few new friends and be less lonely, but God's plan for community has a much greater purpose.

▷ If you don't know what to do, a good place to start is to get off your hiney and just do something!

▷ God's master plan to save the world is . . . us.

MAIN GOAL: Ignite your women's call to missions both big and small, macro and micro, and the emphasize the joy of being sent out by Jesus, in the company of others.

1. OPEN

Begin by reviewing the personal study from last week. Here are some suggested places to focus as you review:

▷ Though the Great Commission is indeed Great and big and overwhelming, discuss the ways Jesus scaled it down so it could be manageable for his people.

▷ Can you see how even small tasks and goals (even fun or silly ones) contribute to a sense of mission and togetherness?

▷ Discuss the "Master Plan." What sticks out to you the most?

▷ Have women share their drawings from Project 1.

▷ What are your reactions to Ephesians 4:14–16?

▷ What else stood out to you from the lesson and Scripture that you need to learn, treasure, and/or apply?

2. SEE

Watch the video for Session 6, "Shared Mission."

3. ASK

Transition to the Conversation cards to continue your discussion. The cards for this week are labeled "Session 6" on the front. Lead women to choose, answer, and discuss the questions on the cards. (You can review the instructions for using the cards in "SESSION FORMAT" on page 172.)

4. CLOSE

Share a personal experience you've had while on mission with others. Allow the women to share similar stories. If a member of your group is having difficulty with this idea or facing anxiety about it, take a moment to surround her and pray for her.

"He called the twelve and began to send them out two by two". (Mark 6:7)

SESSION 7

CONSISTENCY

MAIN IDEA: When we stay, we grow. Staying, showing up, not quitting, fighting for each other, is the way to reconciliation.

Here are some general goals and thoughts for your time together this session:

> Explore the concept of reconciliation, between us and God, and with each other

> Awaken the craving for a staying, growing, consistent community instead of running when things get hard.

> Discuss the "one anothers" that keep coming up in the Bible.

> Explore the similarities between God's vision for community in Genesis and the one in Revelation

> Arm your women with tools for conflict resolution

We might want to bolt, but staying—consistency—is the way forward to deep community.

MAIN GOAL: Reinforce the bravery it will take to not only start and try new things to reclaim community, but to stick with them and be consistent—and watch them grow.

1. OPEN

Begin by reviewing the personal study from last week. Here are some suggested places to focus as you review:

> Talk about times you've bolted, or situations that make you want to bolt.

> Discuss what makes us edgy about facing conflict, and what tools we can use to face it well.

> Share your excitements and worries about committing to the people you've identified in Project 2. Encourage one another.

> Share your letters in Project 4. What are you dreaming about in the future?

▷ Ask what else they learned as they studied and interacted with the session and Scripture this week.

2. SEE

Watch the video for Session 7: "CONSISTENCY"

3. ASK

Transition to the Conversation cards to continue your discussion. The cards for this week are labeled "Session 7" on the front. Lead women to choose, answer, and discuss the questions on the cards. (You can review the instructions for using the cards in "SESSION FORMAT" on page 172.)

4. CLOSE

Talk about how our struggles with loneliness and connection are so personal, raw, and real. Emphasize again that everyone in the group is in the same boat, sinners set free from sin but still struggling to make "Earth as it is in heaven" on an earth that is so very broken. Cheer your group on, encouraging them to dare, risk, open up, and continually turn to Jesus and to the Holy Spirit for guidance as they continue to show up for the people in their lives. Invite several women to pray to close your time together.

"Be kind to one another, tenderhearted, forgiving one another, as God in Christ forgave you". (Ephesians 4:32)

We Aren't Supposed to Be This Lonely.

But you don't have to stay there. Let's find your people.

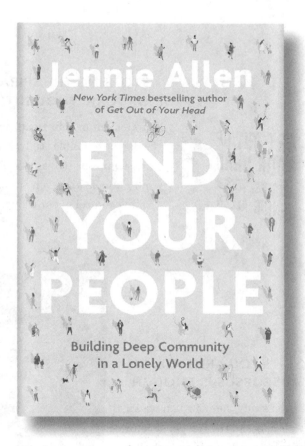

You were created to play, engage, adventure, and explore—with others. In *Find Your People*, you'll discover exactly how to dive into the deep end and experience the full wonder of community. Because while the ache of loneliness is real, it doesn't have to be your reality.

ALSO AVAILABLE FROM JENNIE ALLEN

STOPPING THE SPIRAL OF TOXIC THOUGHTS

In Get Out of Your Head, a six-session, video-based Bible study, Jennie inspires and equips us to transform our emotions, our outlook, and even our circumstances by taking control of our thoughts.

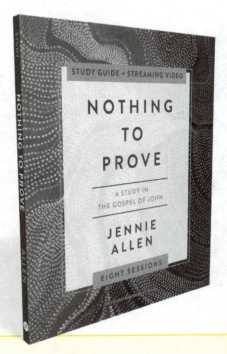

YOU ARE ENOUGH BECAUSE JESUS IS ENOUGH.

In this 8-session study, Jennie Allen walks through key passages in the Gospel of John that demonstrate how Jesus is enough. We don't have to prove anything because Jesus has proven everything.

IDENTIFY THE THREADS OF YOUR LIFE

In this DVD-based study using the story of Joseph, Jennie explains how his suffering, gifts, story, and relationships fit into the greater story of God—and how your story can do the same.

THE PLACES WE GET STUCK & THE GOD WHO SETS US FREE

Stuck is an eight-session Bible study experience leading women to the invisible struggles that we fight and to the God who has to set us free.

CHASING AFTER THE HEART OF GOD

Chase is a seven-session Bible study experience to discover the heart of God and what it is exactly He wants from us through major events in the life of David, and the Psalms.